michael  S.

WAR GAMES

The Author discussing a war game with Brigadier Peter Young

WAR GAMES TABLE WITH BATTLE

DONALD F. FEATHERSTONE

WAR GAMES

Battles and Manœuvres with Model Soldiers

STANLEY PAUL
London

STANLEY PAUL & CO. LTD
3 Fitzroy Square, London W1

AN IMPRINT OF THE HUTCHINSON GROUP

London Melbourne Sydney Auckland
Wellington Johannesburg Cape Town
and agencies throughout the world

First published May 1962
Reprinted December 1965
Reprinted August 1967
Reprinted November 1968
Reprinted October 1970
Reprinted January 1972

Printed in Great Britain by litho on antique wove paper
by Anchor Press, and bound by Wm. Brendon,
both of Tiptree, Essex
ISBN 0 09 064901 X

Contents

Illustrations

MAPS

Foreword

by

BRIGADIER PETER YOUNG,
D.S.O., M.C., M.A., F.S.A., F.R.HIST.S. (RETD.)

As DONALD FEATHERSTONE shows in the opening chapter of his book, war games have a long history. Indeed, one could say that practically any military exercise is a form of war game. I remember taking part in many several years before I joined the Army, often with the late Captain J. C. Sachs of Bushey, Hertfordshire, who had worked out an elaborate set of rules to cover the period of the First World War. My own preference is for eighteenth-century warfare—the musket period, roughly speaking 1702-1815. Then the three arms—horse, foot and guns—ruled the field, ranges were relatively short, and therefore it is relatively easy to evolve simple rules. Later, and particularly in the twentieth century, things became so complicated that it is hard to devise rules which really relate to what happens in warfare!

As this book shows, most hardened war gamers have their own rules. This can be confusing! But it doesn't matter much so long as the rules really relate to the characteristics of the weapons at the various periods. This is the important point. Since the success of one's tactics depends upon the use of ground and of weapons, there is no need for elaborate rules covering morale, or compelling the player to manœuvre in the formations employed in the days of Frederick the Great or Napoleon. The 'General' can sort out his formations for himself, and therein lies the pleasure of the game.

Quite apart from the amusement that can be derived from

9

a war game, it can teach valuable military lessons, for it familiarizes the players with the methods of war, such as building up a reserve or attempting to take the enemy by surprise. The great German victory of Tannenberg (26–30 August 1914) was planned in accordance with the solution of a similar situation in a war game played by the German general staff in 1912!

Donald Featherstone, who has the advantage that he himself saw active service in Italy during the Second World War, has made a thorough study of war games. His lively and straightforward book is the first addition to the literature of the subject since the days of H. G. Wells, and will, I trust, appeal to a wide circle of readers.

PETER YOUNG

Preface

THIS is an age of 'Do-It-Yourself' in which every man, aided
by kits, mechanical devices and reams of instructions, attempts
personally to carry out technical tasks usually performed by
experts. This book can be said to enter into the spirit of things
in that it contains advice and instructions enabling frustrated
ex-lance-corporals and disillusioned second lieutenants to pro-
mote themselves to the rank of general and brilliantly command
valiant armies.

To claim that the contents are completely original would be
false, the keener brains of those brilliant writers (and obviously
eternal boys) H. G. Wells and Robert Louis Stevenson had
devised ingenious methods of making miniature war long
before I was born. However, it is modestly claimed that this
volume 'streamlines' war games as played by Wells in the
light of modern conditions and supplies of war-games
accessories. Herein is contained the basic material in the form
of rules and advice that will enable very enjoyable games to be
carried on, with no bloodshed, widows, orphans or nuclear
weapons.

Many of the ideas and suggestions given here have been
gathered together from other players, because war gamers are
generous, helpful people who willingly let their pet rules be
freely publicized. They have been co-ordinated, tried, per-
fected and polished so as to give a realistic, fast and interesting
game. They leave great gaps for personal improvement, and
many of them, in fact, have been altered by the author since
this book was commenced. Therein lies the charm of war
gaming, it is an adaptable pursuit that can be moulded to
the temperament and character of the player—for example,
one well-known player shows an admirable side to his

nature by having the most humane rules covering prisoners of war, whereas most players just can't be bothered about them!

It should not be thought that the only types of war games are those described herein, i.e. ancient, horse-and-musket and modern. There are players greatly enjoying games between small numbers of Settlers and Redskins; naval warfare ranging from massed battles between triremes and biremes to heady affairs with battleships, aircraft carriers and submarines; air war involving the flimsy biplanes of World War One; to say nothing of the most popular Napoleonic campaigns.

The pleasure does not begin and end with the actual playing of the war game. There are many pleasant hours to be spent in making model soldiers, painting them, constructing terrain, carrying out research into battles, tactics and uniforms by means of browsing in museums and bookshops, correspondence with fellow-collectors in many countries of the world and, finally, collating descriptions of your battles with drawings and photographs. All these enterprises go towards building up a big debt of gratitude to those many friends and willing helpers who have nursed the author along since his early collecting days—the first friend who more or less did the necessary introductions to the game, Tony Bath of Southampton, Roy Blackman of the same town, Bill Gunson of Kuwait, Charles Grant of Dover, Archie Cass of London, Major Carl Reavley of the Aden Protectorate Levies, Brigadier Peter Young of Sandhurst, Ed Saunders of Taunton, Lionel Tarr of Bristol, Newell Chamberlin of St Louis, U.S.A., Jack Scruby of California and hordes of others who will forgive the omission of their names.

Thanks are also due to Ken Baker, who so patiently took the photographs for the book—knowing little or nothing of the hobby, Ken could have been irritatingly puzzled at times by the apparently purposeless movement of soldiers for 'the next shot' but he bore it all with good humour and may yet be converted into a war gamer!

The hobby and its players have done much to enrich the life of the author, whilst possibly taking up a considerable amount of time and money that his wife might well have felt could have been applied more usefully—but, like the small, lead soldiers, she is silent and tactful!! War games have brought a glimpse of pageantry and colour to the lives of their adherents, and put a merciful glamour over war, thus giving it a quality that it has never deserved and which, in the light of modern events, it is never likely to achieve.

The tremendous forward march of war gaming since this book was published eight years ago has been beyond my wildest expectations. In Great Britain alone, for every single war gamer fighting battles in 1962, there is now a hundred. There are available numerous types of model soldiers, magazines, books, accessories—and rules! It is very warming to feel that the original publication of this book provided much of that impetus.

DONALD F. FEATHERSTONE

1970

1

What are War Games?

THE very first war game could have been played in prehistoric times, when a young, skin-clad boy, sitting outside the family cave, found some pine-cones. Lining them up in an irregular formation, he called them 'that tribe across the river who are always stealing our food' and began savagely to decimate them by throwing rocks into their ranks! It is quite possible that the children of the more civilized of the early countries were given crude model soldiers made of carved wood, moulded clay or even metal. It is quite logical to presuppose that those children, tiring of merely standing their soldiers in lines, began to match one group against another and throw, or otherwise propel, stones and marbles at them. Individual combats, such as the children witnessed in the gladiatorial arena, were reproduced when two soldiers of clay faced each other and, in some way, were made to fight until one fell and the other remained triumphant.

We could assume, with equal likelihood of being correct, that military giants such as Hannibal and Alexander used small representations of their soldiers and mock-ups of the terrain over which they expected to battle made up in the sandy soil on which they were camped. How many flanking movements, or oblique orders of battle, to name but two military manœuvres known to that day, were planned thus and later used to the confusion of the enemy?

History reveals in fascinating glimpses that military leaders have used models to plan battles and to teach the science of strategy and tactics. It is known that in the seventeenth century the young French dauphins were taught in this fashion how eventually to command the magnificent French armies, the flower of European soldiery at that time. Frederick the Great used models, as did Napoleon, and the Prussians used *Kriegspiel* to plan the tactics that smashed the French in 1870 and also enabled the Germans almost to reach Paris in 1914. In the *Illustrated War News* for 25 November 1914 there appears a drawing showing a number of serious-looking young men bending over a large-scale map; underneath appears the caption:

'Why not teach Kitchener's Army this during evenings at the Training Centres? Playing the War Game "Bellum". Never was it more opportune that such a revival as that of the war game shown should be instituted, especially as it is desired to keep Kitchener's Army fittingly amused and employed during the evenings while the men are in training. "Bellum" is thoroughly scientific. In earlier games every player could see the whole map and learn the configuration of the country. In "Bellum" this is avoided by movable screens which make invisible such movements as in actual warfare the enemy could not see. By means of coloured ribbons representing rivers, railways, roads, etc., red string marking the contours of the country, and conventional signs for woods, lakes, villages, and so forth, a map of any country can be made on the white cloth of a table. Killed and wounded are calculated by an umpire.'

So it is extremely likely that war games played their part in World War I, whilst the author recalls, with some pleasure, a fascinating hut at Bovington Camp, Dorset, in the Second World War, where miniature tanks were made to move over realistic countryside, being made mobile by the movement of magnets underneath the table!

But all war games have not been solely for the purpose of discovering new ways of destroying one's fellow-men—there can be few boys who have not received, with shining eyes, the birthday and Christmas presents of boxes of model soldiers— usually made by the famous British soldier-makers, William

Britains of London. And those boys will invariably have tried to play some very elementary form of war game with their few soldiers, until that day when they have acquired lots of them and discovered, in the local library, a worn copy of H. G. Wells's book *Little Wars*. When that book has once been pored over, all games with model soldiers take on a new lustre, attain a standard and level of amusement and intelligence that far surpasses all previous attempts at war gaming.

War games appear to have fascinated men of letters, although in some cases the men themselves possessed the most peaceful natures. Of such a type was Robert Louis Stevenson, who devised and played a most intricate and prolonged mimic war in an attic during his convalescent days in Davos in 1880–3. Lloyd Osbourne's 'Stevenson at Play', published in *Scribner's Magazine* in December 1898, contains the fullest and most fascinating details of the game, which in its entirety is far more complicated than anything described in this book! It is recorded that G. K. Chesterton found war games intensely interesting, and the fashion for literary giants to fight with model soldiers was upheld by yet another famous writer-to-be who also has achieved fame in other directions. As a boy, this man had the whole procedure on a most business-like basis, and very likely used the knowledge gained by fighting on the playroom floor to great advantage in later life. The chief amusements of Sir Winston Churchill's boyhood were his model soldiers. He commanded an army and his brother Jack took the enemy. They had fifteen hundred men each, organized as an infantry division with a cavalry brigade. The young Winston had a quick brain even as a boy, because his brother Jack was allowed to have only coloured troops and he was permitted no artillery, whilst Winston's army could muster eighteen field guns!

It is recorded that Winston's father, Lord Randolph Churchill, came like a field marshal on a visit of inspection. All the troops were drawn up, ready for immediate attack. Lord Randolph spent twenty minutes inspecting the scene. He then turned towards his son and asked him if he would like to become a soldier. The boy thought it would be splendid to command an army, so he said 'Yes' at once—it was a fateful

B

answer, his father took him at his word and Sir Winston was henceforth committed to an army career.

But it is H. G. Wells who can be considered to be the founder of war games as they are fought today. His rules form the basis for practically every set of conditions under which people of all countries fight with model soldiers. In 1912 H. G. Wells, known widely as an author of what would today probably be called science-fiction and with views far in advance of his day in the fields of aviation and social conditions, wrote two articles for the *Windsor Magazine* of December 1912 and January 1913—entitled 'Little Wars'. As a direct result of these articles, Frank Palmer, the publisher, suggested to Wells that a book might well be written on the subject of boys' games. Accordingly, Wells presented himself at the publisher's offices in Bloomsbury. Another author, R. Thurston Hopkins, was discussing a book with Palmer when Wells arrived, and with Wells were box after box of bricks, trees and soldiers. These were spread all over the floor, and for the next three hours Wells crawled about on hands and knees, extolling the virtues of the game, eventually leaving with a contract in his pocket and an exhausted Palmer, Hopkins and staff behind him!

When the book appeared it bore on the title page the following apt summing-up of the whole background of war gaming:

'LITTLE WARS—a Game for Boys from Twelve Years of Age to One Hundred and Fifty and for that more Intelligent sort of Girl who likes Boys' Games and Books.'

Wells points out that the book describes '. . . a game that may be played by two, four or six amateurish persons in an afternoon and evening with toy soldiers'.

Part of the fun of being a war gamer lies in the making of one's own soldiers as distinct from purchasing figures of different sizes obtainable from makers in various parts of the world. This sometimes involves making, initially, a 'master-model' from which the mould is made, which can then be used to cast further models in molten metal. Perhaps not quite so scrupulously, some collectors will buy one solitary figure of a particular type from which they will make a mould and then cast many more soldiers, all more or less exact replicas of the 'commercial' figure originally purchased. The amateur model-soldier maker is almost invariably a perfectionist, and goes to endless trouble in order to ensure that his small figures are correctly equipped and painted. He carries out patient research into old books and prints; haunts museums, libraries and secondhand-book shops seeking authentic illustrations of the particular soldier he is making at the time. Collectors assist one another freely and gladly—if John Smith of London cannot discover the exact uniform worn by the Voltigeurs of the French Imperial Guard in 1870 then Elmer C. Rudd of Chicago, Illinois, in the United States of America, will be only too pleased to let him know—by airmail!

Collectors can be found who specialize in almost any conceivable period of history, from Ancient Britons to atomic warfare. Campaigns are conducted in which Roman fights Carthaginian, Greek battles with Persian warrior, the Wars of the Roses resume their bloody course across the fifteenth-century English countryside, the Cavaliers have another attempt to beat the Roundheads, Red Indians aid white-uniformed French to fight the British Redcoats in the forests of America and Canada and, approaching by far the most popular period, the French take on almost the rest of Europe in the Peninsula and over the entire Continent. Napoleon plans to defeat Wellington at Waterloo and sometimes does so! The Crimean War seems to hold little attraction for war gamers, but the soon-to-follow American Civil War presents a fascination that is increasing daily—this was the first of the modern wars with trains, telegraphs, breech-loading guns and armoured warships. The Franco-Prussian War of 1870 has some adherents in Great Britain but far more on the Continent. Its troops still wear many gaily coloured uniforms and the battles are capably described in many easily obtainable books. The colonial campaigns of Great Britain in the latter part of the nineteenth century make interesting war games. The tribesmen of the North-West Frontier form impressive opponents, as do the Zulus of the 1879 war. The Boer War presents interesting problems for the war-games table with its large preponderance of cavalry on the Boer side. Few collectors seem interested in World War I, although there is much of value to be found in the battles of 1914 and early 1915, before the war bogged down in a mass of trench warfare—a fasinating little campaign can be made of the German East Africa fighting in which native troops can be used. And so we approach the last war, if one omits Korea—many collectors find World War II very much worth while. One enthusiast is re-fighting the German attack on Russia and is, at the time of writing, making a model of the city of Stalingrad on the scale of ⅛ inch equals 6 feet!

For the player who finds nothing of interest in this list, there are imaginary campaigns that he may fight without limit. He can form his imaginary world, with continents and countries each of which will make war on its neighbour on the slightest pretext. The French find themselves involved in wars with America, the British take on the Russians in period 1900, and great wars take place between countries who, at the actual period in time when the campaign is deemed to be taking place, were the very best of friends in real life!

Therein lies one of the fascinations of war gaming—one can remake history to suit one's own ideas, can alter the complete trend of events by re-fighting a major battle such as Waterloo and making the French win it—imagine what would have been the result if the French *had* won in 1815 and then see just how powerful the war gamer can make himself. Not for him the restrictions and frustrations of pacts and power-bloc—he can make his own and break his own without causing a single wife to be made a widow or child to be rendered fatherless, because there is no one braver than the lead soldier without any lead wives or lead children!

It will possibly amaze the layman to be told that it is relatively easy to obtain model soldiers in any of the periods previously mentioned; that one can acquire armies of soldiers of any country, in any period and with the men cast in any desired position of belligerency. Largely manufactured in France and Germany, small war-games figures known as 'Flats' can be purchased cheaply and, in fact, form almost the sole type of war-games figures used in those countries. Otherwise, if the collector does not fancy these two-dimensional-type figures, which are almost flat stamped pieces appearing as thin vertical lines when viewed from the front or rear, then he has two alternatives. Firstly, he can specialize in a period for which it is possible easily to obtain figures—this particularly applies to the Napoleonic period and the American Civil War, to name but two—or, secondly, he can pick any other period he desires and then turn out his own soldiers tailor-made to that particular era by making them himself with moulds (which he will also have to make) and casting them in various sorts of lead alloys. Instead of this onerous chore, he can purchase figures of any other period and 'convert' them by adding helmets, packs, gaiters, etc., by means of glueing into position shapes of these items cast separately in lead or by moulding them into shape in plastic wood or barbola paste. They are then glued into position. Plastic figures are particularly easy to convert because one merely shaves off the parts that are not needed, using a razor blade, and then builds up fresh contours with plastic wood as already mentioned.

There is a great deal of satisfaction in making one's own armies, either in their entirety or by conversions. Few war-games players seem to buy their figures ready-made and already painted and then merely take them into action—nearly every one at least paints his own figures even if he does not actually make them. In fact, it is by far the rule rather than the exception that most of the smaller-sized war-games type of figures are sold unpainted.

Having established that it is necessary to have a collection of model soldiers, divided into at least two armies, before one can fight war games—what else is required? It falls naturally into place that some form of battlefield on which to fight the war game must be sought. This can be of almost any size, dependent upon the numbers of troops involved and the magnitude of the game concerned. It can be a baize-topped card table or squared pieces of cardboard laid down on an ordinary dining-room table, or it can take the form of a vast tray of hardboard 10 feet by 6 feet in which sand is placed from which hills, roads, rivers, etc., are made, duly coloured and embellished with scaled-down houses, bridges, trees and the like. Most war gamers have, in the backs of their minds, an ambition to have a war-games table of gigantic proportions— say 18 feet by 6 feet—in order that they can achieve wide flanking movements and generally manœuvre on the grand scale! This is all very well in theory but somewhat difficult in practice because war games invariably seem (gregariously) to spend most of their time in one section of the table; rarely is a large proportion of the terrain used. The width of the table should not be much more than 5 feet because it is extremely difficult to lean over a wider table and move your troops in the middle. Many of the assumed advantages of being able to move largely on the table come to naught on account of time— most war gamers find it necessary for various reasons to begin and end their battle on the same day. This becomes very difficult to achieve when troops are wandering around an area of perhaps 80 to 100 square feet.

This mention of the time factor leads on to another facet of war gaming: the tailoring of the game to suit the players, the terrain, the time available and the ultimate objectives involved. Briefly, this means that the type of game will be different according to whether it is played on a permanent or a temporary set-up—one adopts different outlooks if the table on which one is playing is required for tea in perhaps an hour's time rather than it being an elaborate sand table in a room set aside for the hobby. As will be seen later, terrains can vary amazingly and can be literally assembled in a matter of minutes, or it may be the work of hours to lay out a most realistic simulation of an agricultural area, for example. The game that is being played might be merely a single contest between two small armies—much in the nature of an impromptu game of chess—or it may be part of a campaign that has initially begun on maps and includes supply problems, attrition and many other factors common to real warfare. The former game involves only one army beating another and often ends up with one force having five men left bravely fighting off the seven remaining soldiers of the enemy. But the battle that forms part of a campaign is far more interesting and will have its fascination resting in the fact that one side can lose the battle and still have remaining more than half its troops (as would happen in real life), solely because a vital crossroads or a bridge has been captured and, lines of communication having been cut, the unlucky army has to retreat and save itself for the next battle in the campaign.

The schoolboy, when first presented with toy soldiers, will play a primitive form of war game by lining them up and firing a cannon at them, the winner generally being the side that loses the least men. But that simple game does not satisfy him for long. He soon wishes to make charges, defend forts and conduct skilful retreats, but lacks the know-how. So he devises some very elementary rules and his game begins to take on some semblance of realism. Most war gamers have progressed a long way since schooldays, although some great enthusiasts still have to finish their maths homework before fighting their battle, and these older devotees have devised systems of rules under which they fight that cover most of the eventualities of warfare. The general idea of most sets of rules—and there are almost as many rule books as there are war gamers—is to give the game the greatest possible realism, to permit tactics and practices with model soldiers that conform to those used in real warfare of the period selected by the fighters. It is generally considered, however, that the basis of most sets of rules lies in those suggested by H. G. Wells in *Little Wars*, with the principal exception that few, if any, war gamers actually fire cannon at their troops—having spent many hours making and painting model soldiers it is a foolhardy collector who permits them to have pieces of metal rod fired forcibly in their general direction!

It is not within the scope of this volume to discuss the theory that playing with military toys tends to encourage a warlike spirit—a charge that is periodically given an airing and has been levelled for the past hundred years with such effect that the Allied Armies of Occupation in Germany after World War II banned all such evidence of militarism, restricting toy-makers to such innocuous items as cowboys and Indians! Perhaps there is an even more meritorious service that war games can render mankind, other than giving many hours of pleasure. As H. G. Wells said:

'The best possible cure for wars is to put this prancing monarch and that silly scaremonger, those excitable patriots and that adventurer, into one vast Temple of War, with plenty of little trees and houses to knock down and cities and fortresses and unlimited model soldiers—tons, cellars full of them—and let them lead their own lives there away from ours. Indeed you only have to play at Little Wars three or four times to realize just what a blundering thing Great War must be. Great War is, at present, I am convinced, not only the most expensive game in the Universe, but it is a game out of all proportion.'

2

Model Soldiers for War Games

MOST war-games players select their armies from one of the
following five types:

1. 54 mm solids
2. 40 mm solids
3. 30 mm solids
4. oo gauge solids (20 and 25 mm)
5. Flats.

There are other sizes which have their supporters but
undoubtedly the most popular war-games figures today are the
20 and 25 mm figures which are obtainable made both in
plastic and metal.

The 54 mm figure is the well-known size that we usually
collected in our boyhood, and which were almost invariably
made by Britains. Although they are the figures mentioned and
used in the illustrations contained in Wells's *Little Wars* they
are not often used in war games, at least not after the player has
had the opportunity of using smaller figures! The terrain has to
be extremely spacious, such as an outdoor game in the garden,
and the number of troops involved necessarily has to be much
smaller than when using soldiers of 30 mm, for example.
However, if any reader sincerely wishes to fight his battles with
these large figures he can do little better than visit his local toy-
shop or one of the larger shops such as Hamleys of Regent

Street, London, where he will find a selection of these larger figures made by Britains. Unfortunately they are now all plastic as are the 54 mm figures of other makers that can be obtained at cheaper prices in Woolworths.

There are some players using 40 mm figures of their own manufacture, feeling that this size soldier still possesses some of the detail and accuracy of the larger 54 mm figure whilst being that much smaller and able to be handled on the war-games table. Commercially they are difficult to obtain with the possible exception of the plastic figures made in Germany under the name of Elastolin.

It was the availability of the 30 mm solid or round figure that gave war gaming the impetus that began it on its road to the flourishing hobby it is today. It was soon realised that these figures, about $1\frac{1}{8}$ inch in height, were large enough to possess accurate detail and yet could be used in large numbers on the average-sized war-games table. They were not particularly expensive and could be obtained in a large variety of types, armies and periods through English agents of the Swedish African Engineers of South Africa—the figures were generally known to collectors as S.A.E. figures. They came in boxes of six infantry or three cavalry for about 4s a box and the range of available figures was very wide, covering the American War of Independence, Napoleonics, Austro-Italian War, Franco-Prussian War, American Civil War, through World Wars One and Two. These figures have been out of production for some years and their commercial counterparts are those obtainable from manufacturers such as Jack Scruby, Tradition, Willie, Oscar, Miniature Figurines etc.

In recent years the war games situation has been revolutionized by the boxes of oo gauge plastic figures marketed by Airfix at a very low price. The range is constantly if tardily increasing and now offers the war gamer figures that can be used in many periods of warfare from Rome to the present day. Perhaps the greatest blessing of these little plastic figures lies in the fact that they are so readily convertible into almost any other type of soldier desired. Regular articles in *Airfix Magazine* describe these methods of conversion, in addition the subject is

fully discussed in the book *Military Modelling* by Donald
Featherstone (Kaye and Ward, London, 1970) and by specially
written articles in the magazine *War-Gamer's Newsletter*.

Lastly, we come to Flats, already mentioned as being
available in the most amazing variety of periods, types and
positions. These are largely made in Germany and are not too
easy to obtain by the English collector unless he has a contact
in Germany! Flats are not to everyone's taste, being flat as
their name suggests and rather unimposing when viewed from
the front or rear—but from the side they present an un-
paralleled appearance, being accurate, detailed and of the
highest quality in their engraving. They are relatively cheap in
price and have a big selling point in the fact that they are light
in weight and easily transportable, so that armies can be taken
to an opponent's house when 'playing away'. It is quite true
to say that there is no army or soldier that one can name that
cannot be obtained in flat and in any desired position, including
wounded or killed! They are roughly 30 mm in size and, if
confirmation is required of their quality, they can be seen in the
wonderful dioramas of British battles in the United Services
Museum in London.

The commercial sources of supply for war-games figures
having been covered, an infinitely more interesting position
appears in which the collector makes his own soldiers. Not for
him the ready-made offerings, restricting his choice of period
and type of figures besides regularly taking considerable sums
of money from his pocket. The ingenious collector is able to
build up armies of any period, soldiers in any desired stance or
position, at a fraction of the cost of the bought article and to
gain an ultimate sense of satisfaction coming from genuine
achievement. Do not let it be thought that this is done easily,
there is a considerable amount of sheer effort, of onerous and
repetitive labour, before the little figures are detailed and res-
plendent in their correctly coloured uniforms. The real enthusiast takes this work for granted, his labours are those of love
and the results far more treasured than any commercial
collection.

Making one's own soldiers involves the use of some sort of

a mould in which the figures are cast. In almost every case this mould will have to be made by the collector, as the only available commercial moulds are of large, semi-flat figures of a mediocre nature. The easiest material of which a mould can be made is plaster of Paris, but this type of mould does not permit the manufacture of figures with deep insets, known as undercuts, as such figures cannot be removed from the mould after casting without irretrievably damaging the mould. Thus the home maker is restricted to making flat or round figures of a semi-flat nature without undercuts. It is possible to make plaster moulds consisting of three or four parts that will turn out figures with the deepest undercuts, but their manufacture is a highly complicated and skilled business, far beyond the capabilities of the average collector.

It would take many pages to fully explain the processes involved in making plaster moulds so, necessarily, guidance in this field must be brief. Once the elementary intricacies have been overcome it is not a difficult business, and the maker will soon be able to reason out more elaborate and delicate projects.

To begin the simplest form of mould, the following items are required:

 1 lb plasticine (colour immaterial)
 7 lb tin plaster of Paris (obtainable from art shops)
 Model soldier to be used as 'master' figure.

This figure must be of a simple nature, fairly flat and without undercuts such as the arms held out in front of the body bearing a rifle. First, the figure must be imbedded in a slab of plasticine about half an inch in thickness, it is essential that the figure is imbedded *exactly* half its thickness, the plasticine being built up around the figure with a penknife point so that this situation prevails. Next, build a wall of plasticine around the slab so that a box is formed—with the slab (and its imbedded figure) as the base, four sides each about one and a half inches in height and the top remaining open. This box must be completely watertight.

Mix a quantity of plaster of Paris sufficient almost to fill the box. It should be of a thick, creamy consistency and, to obtain the best results, the plaster should be of the fine type used by artists or dentists' technicians. Before actually pouring the plaster into the box, make two impressions with the end of a pencil or the rounded end of a fountain pen in the plasticine slab holding the figure, this will ensure that this half of the mould, when dry, will have two 'keys' arising from its surface, which will 'lock' with the second half of the mould when they are fitted together. To avoid air bubbles, pour the mixture very carefully into the box and allow to stand for at least half an hour whilst the plaster hardens.

When the plaster has hardened, gently peel off the plasticine walls and base, this will leave a block of plaster in which the figure will be imbedded. Using a penknife, ease the figure carefully from the plaster, first running the knife point around the outline of the figure. Brush all loose pieces of plaster off both the figure and mould-half and then repeat the process of building a plasticine wall around the plaster block, which on this occasion becomes the base of the box with the impression of the figure uppermost. Press the plasticine under the bottom of the plaster block to ensure that the box is watertight. Place the cleaned-up figure into the impression formed in the plaster block and then brush lightly a fine film of olive oil over the whole surface of the plaster block and the figure; this ensures that the two halves separate when dry.

Mix a similar quantity of plaster as before and pour gently into the box, leave to dry for at least half an hour. When hard, gently insert a penknife blade between the two plaster halves, after stripping off the plasticine wall, and prise them apart, the olive oil having prevented them from fusing together. The mould will then consist of two halves, one half with the impression of the figure contained in it and the other half with the actual figure still imbedded therein. Using the same technique as before, carefully ease the figure from the plaster, brush off all loose pieces of plaster from both mould-halves and place them in a warm place to dry. It is essential that five to seven days are allowed for the mould to dry out completely, as it is extremely dangerous to pour molten metal into a plaster mould that is still damp, the moisture causing the molten metal to be forcibly expelled via the pouring hole with a detrimental effect to the ceiling, or the maker's face if he happens to be bending over the mould at the time!

When the drying period has elapsed, fit the two halves of the mould together to check that they correspond: they should fit tightly. Take them apart and mark on each half-mould a 'run-in' through which the molten metal will be poured. This is a wedge-shaped piece cut out of each half of the mould running from the outer surface of the mould down to the under part of the base of the figure. When the mould-halves are put together this cut-out 'run-in' should present a small hole on the outside of the complete mould, getting smaller as it proceeds inwards to the base of the model. With a penknife point, score lines in the plaster from all projecting parts of the soldier, such as from the hat-top, rifle-end and shoulders, etc. Carry these lines out to the outer surface of the mould as they are the channels through which the air will be expelled when the molten metal is poured into the mould.

The type of metal to be used in casting the figure has now to be considered. It is not good enough to get hold of an old piece of lead piping, melt it down, and expect to get other than a soft, ill-defined figure. To obtain a clear, well-defined figure, a hard metal must be used, but it will be brittle and easily broken. Therefore, a combination of metals is required that will give reasonable definition to the model and will be, at the same time, soft enough to be bent or filed. The easiest combination is undoubtedly one part of tinsmith's solder to two parts of plumber's solder; whilst a cheaper and reasonably satisfactory method is to use two parts of ordinary lead and one part of printer's type, which can usually be quite easily obtained from the local printer, who usually has a considerable surplus of cuttings and small pieces.

Heat the metal in an old saucepan or ladle with a pouring

lip. Do not let it 'boil' for long periods as this makes it 'lazy' and it will not run satisfactorily into the mould. A scum or dross will sometimes form on top of the molten metal; this must be skimmed off as it impedes pouring and spoils the casting. As the best results are obtained from a heated mould, it should be warmed up before casting commences. Hold the faces of the mould over a candle flame so that a film of soot is deposited on both the mould faces and the impressions contained therein. This facilitates removal of the casting and prevents the mould from crumbling.

Fasten the two halves of the mould together with a clamp, stand the mould on a number of thicknesses of newspaper with the opening of the pour-in hole uppermost. Hold the ladle well above the pour-in hole and allow the stream of molten metal to drop down into the hole, thus by its own weight the metal forces its way into the many crevices of the impressions in the plaster. Allow the metal to harden for a few minutes, then carefully open the mould, remembering that the metal is still extremely hot and capable of inflicting a nasty burn. With a pair of pincers, gently remove the gleaming casting from its bed, holding it by its base. This is a most delicate operation because, at this point, it is extremely easy to break off pieces of the plaster clinging to the casting, so that, after two or three pourings, the figure will begin to emerge in a mis-shapen state surrounded by large pieces of metal 'flash'.

Ideally, it is best to cast only four or five figures per session, as it is the intense heat that causes the moulds to break up. With care, it is possible to obtain about twenty reasonable figures from a mould before it becomes too damaged to produce a worthwhile soldier. The casting as it emerges from the mould will require filing and generally cleaning up to make it ready for painting. This part of model-soldier making is the most discouraging angle, as it is tedious and laborious. The figure should be fixed into a vice and worked upon with a selection of fine rat-tail and model-maker's files to take off the unfortunately inevitable 'flash'.

There are other ways of making model soldiers in moulds,

mostly aimed at eliminating the bugbear of 'flash'. Moulds can be made out of reclaimable synthetic rubber compounds which give a flexible mould that peels off the completed casting. These moulds are not suitable to use with molten metals of high temperature and the only suitable metal is Wood's Metal which melts at the temperature of boiling water but is so highly priced that it makes the whole process most uneconomical. A firm known as the Midland Silicones Ltd, of 68 Knightsbridge, London, S.W.1, are now turning out a siliconized rubber compound that will take temperatures of over 400°F, and early experiments, using the material in the same way as the plaster-of-Paris technique already described, indicate that this stuff may well be the answer to the problem. It is also possible to make figures from flexible rubber moulds, using a mixture of resin and metal filler. The castings turn out exactly like normal metal castings, can be filed and worked in the same way, but take twelve hours to harden and cannot be removed from the mould in less than that time.

There is a third method of acquiring the type of soldiers required by the collector and that is to convert figures from their original state into the type and positions required. This conversion business can be a complicated affair or of a relatively simple nature, dependent upon how high a standard of the finished article is required—but war-games players do not really need figures that are works of art. If the collector confines his activities to removing the parts of a figure that he does not require, such as a pack or a shako, and replacing them with alternative structures moulded in plastic wood, he will find that quite reasonable results are easily obtained. By means of this method, headgear can be altered, packs added, rolled blankets placed on top of packs or slung round the model's shoulders, ordinary trousers turned into baggy Zouave pants, overcoats added, etc. If plastic figures are being altered the superfluous parts are removed with a razor blade and moulded plastic-wood additions glued in place.

The conversion of figures can be tackled in many ways: By converting a number of identical figures to some other type, thus forming out of American Civil War-type men a regiment of French infantry, for example. Or by converting a single figure into whatever is required and then making a mould, using your converted figure as the master-model, finally casting as many as required of your new figure.

The position of the arms or legs of a figure can easily be altered: in the case of lead figures the limbs can be bent into new positions with pliers, after 'nicking' the limb at the natural joint (i.e. knees and elbows). The position of arms can be altered on lead figures by filing (or otherwise cutting off) the figure's arms at shoulder level, then drilling a hole through the figure at shoulder level from one side of the man to the other. Through this hole thread a piece of thin wire, glueing or soldering it in position. When it is secure it is bent into the desired position, then coated to the appropriate thickness with plastic wood, leaving a short length of wire at the end of the arm on which can be soldered a rifle, sword or whatever weapon the figure carries. Plastic figures can be altered in much the same way, the arms being shaved from the figure with a razor blade, but, instead of passing wire through the figure, press into the shoulders on each side a pin, which is cut off to the required length and duly coated with plastic wood, weapons being soldered on to the snipped-off ends of the pins.

Finally, all soldiers have to be painted to resemble the armies of their period and this can be done crudely or to a highly professional standard. The satisfaction seems to be in strict ratio to the trouble that is taken in this sphere. It is possible that model soldiers look better when painted in matt colours and only parts of them that would normally gleam (such as leather equipment, metal fittings, etc.) painted in gloss paints. But matt paints do not take the constant handling of war games as well as do gloss paints, so the collector must make up his own mind if he wants durability or appearance. There are innumerable model-maker's paints on the market that admirably fit the bill and, as they are obtainable in both matt and gloss, it is possible to combine the two in pleasing fashion.

Artillery and limbers, tanks, etc., can be purchased from the same people who market soldiers, but it is often better to attempt to make one's own or improvise upon already existing

C

models. It is to be hoped that the firms already turning out impressive and cheap model kits of aeroplanes, cars and the like will eventually turn their attentions to artillery of all periods, vehicles of modern origin for World War II battles and other models dear to the heart of the war gamer.

3

How to Lay Out a Battlefield

TO PLAY chess one needs a chessboard; in the same way to fight a war game one requires a battlefield—here the similarity ends. Whereas the board on which chess is played conforms to an international. standard there are never two war-games tables that are identical. The appearance of the terrain on which a war game is waged reflects in many ways the character and personality of the player who laid it out—the quiet, unimaginative player is content to use the dining-room table, duly extended to its full length, with hills made of different-sized pieces of board laid on top of one another. Roads are strips of brown paper and rivers lengths of blue. The flamboyant, aggressive player lays out a dashing terrain. He employs the largest possible table that the room will take and still give space to edge around the board. His hills are high and rugged, formed of sand (because his table lies permanently in his war-games room, long since converted from the guest room), rivers are realistic stretches of blue-green colour lying between deep sandy banks, roads inch dustily in yellow to a far horizon, trees bristle in abundance and villages lie red-roofed on the plains of coloured sand. There are many other variations that follow temperament, but other factors also play a part in the formation of a battlefield, as will be seen.

In the same way as terrains differ so do the types of war games played thereon. The collector of long standing has his large armies complete with all accompanying arms, such as artillery, engineers and transport, so he must naturally be expected to aspire towards an ambitious game with lots of troops and a realistic large terrain. The novice, partly because he knows no other way and partly because he possesses only a few soldiers, will play a small, compact game on a table or the floor. It may well be found that he has not had time to worry about terrain, so he uses books for hills and his houses are made of bricks filched from the children's toy cupboard. The collector may not have sufficient room to attempt anything permanent, so his table has perforce to be one that is erected before the battle and laboriously packed away when his opponent has caught the last bus home. Of course, it is equally possible to enjoy battles played on a card table or on the floor as on the largest, most elaborate sand table in the most lavishly equipped hobby room imaginable—so let us not laugh or view with amusement set-ups less elaborate than our own because the pleasure is not guaranteed to be in strict ratio to the layout's standards.

It is therefore essential that the war gamer gives some thought to the type of terrain he desires; that he weighs up the convenience, the expense, the size of the table in relation to the number of troops he possesses, the material of which it is to be made. Is it to be truly realistic or of an almost 'symbolic' nature? Is it to conform to the battlefields of history or to be 'rigged' so as to give an interesting battle? They are just a few of the salient points that must govern selection of war-games terrains and which will be covered in this chapter.

It is reasonable to assume that the majority of players aspire towards their own war-games room, with their armies lined up in military ranks on shelves round the walls, with military prints and plates covering the remaining wall space and the entire centre of the room occupied by a permanent table of the biggest possible proportions. The size of the table plays a large part in a war gamer's dreams because, however large his table might be, he always has a secret, frustrated feeling that, had it been three feet longer and two feet wider last week, when he fought his last battle, his ambitious outflanking movement would have been possible instead of fizzling out against his opponent's cavalry! All war gamers dream of extensive movements, of complicated manœuvres that take in large expanses of the table, and their own tables never seem to be large enough! Having bared the souls of war gamers, revealed to the layman these secret longings, it is hoped that a sense of true proportion will pervade this discussion from here on!

It is now known that no table is large enough, but the optimum size of the table to give a good game can be estimated. It must permit adequate movement with reasonable-size armies and allow the game to be concluded in a period compatible with the spare time of the players. Time is another factor that is important. Nothing is more frustrating than to have one's opponent guilelessly falling into your best military trap and then find that midnight is striking and the game cannot be concluded because your earlier moves on a large scale took far too long. If one wishes to fight battles that begin and end in an evening, then the terrain must bear some sensible size-relationship to the distances that the rules permit the troops to move and fight in the available time. The writer has tried campaigns in which battles on a huge scale, using over a thousand men a side, have been spread out over four or five evenings. The inevitable snag has been encountered in that those evenings cannot run concurrently but must be spaced out once per week for a period of over a month. During this time interest unfortunately flags.

The table must be large enough to enable flanking movements and wide sweeps to be carried out, although not so extensive that the battle drags wearily through a series of noncombat moves. It must be of a size that permits a variety of realistic terrains to be constructed, not so large as to make it physically difficult to reach the troops in the middle of the table, and of a height from the floor so that bending is not made too difficult during the hours of battle! Experience has shown that these measurements ideally are as follows—length can be anything between 8 feet and 12 feet, width not more than 6 feet, as this appears to be about the maximum width that will enable the player to lean over comfortably and handle his forces when they are fighting grimly right in the middle of the table! The height of the table should be above that of an ordinary table and can be about $3\frac{1}{2}$ feet—unless one has a special table made for the job it is necessary to lift up the table legs on bricks or blocks of wood to achieve this height.

The table itself is best made out of hardboard, strengthened and supported by lengths of 2 in. × 1 in. timber. If it is to be of a portable nature so that it can rest upon the dining-room table, for example, and close up for storage at other times, then it is best hinged in the middle. The writer's own table, originally used in this fashion, is 8 feet by 5 feet when opened out, or 5 feet by 4 feet when packed away—this means that in each case it takes up much the same amount of room as a table-tennis table. This method of construction presupposes that the terrain is to be of any material other than sand—the sand table of the war gamer's dreams is a far more involved affair and will be covered in due course. The hardboard battle-field can rest upon trestles, on the top of a large ordinary table, or on a specially purchased table—the latter refers to a very good 'buy' that may be obtained sometimes from the surplus stores that dot the countryside; they are mess tables from troop-ships and are very strongly constructed affairs about 3 feet wide, 6 feet long, bound in metal and with removable metal legs that screw into place. These tables are immensely strong and will take the sand table also if required—they can be bought for about 25s or so usually.

A sand table gives a wonderfully realistic battlefield and can be made up into any form of hills, valleys, sunken roads, river-beds, wadis, etc., that may be desired. Generally speaking, the model soldiers stand up quite well on the sand, although there is a tendency for them to slide downwards on hillsides or to cause the sand to break away on inclines. If the war gamer gets a kick out of making his own terrain then he will thoroughly enjoy himself with a sand table, which gives an interesting type of terrain but requires a considerable amount of work in initial preparation and can be rather messy, as sand does not always keep in its proper place on the table! The table itself must be a strongly built affair, no hardboard here but planks with very firm support because sand is extremely heavy and requires the firmest possible base. For the same reason it is essential that the supporting table is strong, and, logical but often forgotten, make sure that the room in which the sand table lies has floorboards that will take the weight! The table will need a built-up 'wall' around it, about 6 inches in height at least or in proportion to the depth of sand on the table. This can be anything from 3 to 9 inches in depth, but, again, remember that sand is heavy and a table 9 feet by 6 feet, for example, with sand to the depth of 6 inches, presents a pretty problem in weight. The sand should be fine plasterer's sand and, as it has to be moist at various stages, it is a good idea to line the table top with some form of plastic or linoleum.

To make a terrain on a sand table, first rake the sand until it lies level and then sprinkle it with water, using a watering can. Rake it again, and again water it—by now it will be moist enough to be shaped into the topographical features present on the map from which you are working. Here you can economize on the quantity of sand used by initially building up your hills with pieces of brick, blocks of wood, etc., and then pile the damp sand over them. With a plasterer's trowel, make the hills, roads, river-beds, etc., and firmly pat them into shape until the whole terrain is complete and lying brown and rather like the Libyan Desert in front of you. The next step is to colour the countryside; this is done by one or two different methods. Firstly, one can use a large tin with holes pierced in its bottom: fill it partly with dry powdered distemper or cement-colouring powder, and move it over the damp sand so that the powder rests lightly on top and is gradually and colourfully absorbed into the sand. The other method is to make a mixture of these colouring powders with water, and, again using a sprinkler, cover the terrain with the coloured mixture. First use green, then a brown, with yellow ochre for cornfields and rich brown for ploughed land. The roads can be brushed on with a soft, large brush in light tan, and the rivers are made to appear very realistic by making the river-bed in the sand and then pouring into it, at its highest point, a mixture of green-blue, which, running down, gives the appearance of water. The additional features, such as trees, walls, fences, houses, bridges, etc., will be mentioned later in this chapter.

Almost equally realistic-looking, and certainly much cleaner to make, is the terrain of plasticine, a substance that will make wonderful hills on which model soldiers will stand and climb with no trouble. The baseboard should be painted with a matt green paint, and the hills, roads, rivers, etc., and other salient features, lightly marked in with chalk before beginning to make the terrain. The hills are first made by laying different-shaped and -sized pieces of wood one on top of the other, with corners rounded and edges bevelled so that they form a terraced-type of hill (this alone, without plasticine, makes a very easy and climbable type of hill for more portable terrains). The wooden hills are next covered with thin sheets of mixed green-brown plasticine, made to irregularly rise and fall, to expand out of the routine oval shape of the wood until the modelling with a penknife blade is finally smeared down on to the baseboard, thus 'anchoring' the hill. Rivers and roads can be chalked or coloured on the baseboard, then 'banks' of brown plasticine rolled into strips are smeared with the blade on to the base along the river, blending into green plasticine to represent grass—this gives a defined edge to the road or river which can be kept low, or raised to deep banks. If the maker prefers he can make plasticine terrain of a more permanent nature by building up hills, river or road sections, woods, etc., on pieces of hardboard about 18 inches square. Fitted together, these squares build up into various combinations of terrain, and, using coloured paper covered by cellophane, realistic rivers can be made, but it always seems to be difficult to fit these squares together so that the river runs realistically, usually it looks odd with angled bends!

The criterion of a hill or raised portion of ground on a war-games table is whether or not the soldiers will stand up on it—unless they will do this then the hill is an ornament with no tactical value at all. Thus the most realistic type of hills made from papier mâché are ruled out unless they are of such gradual gradients as to be not really hills at all. This method consists of nailing odd-shaped pieces of wood on to a baseboard. Over these blocks chicken-wire netting is stretched and bent into shapes of rises and declivities and over the top of the wire netting strips of newspaper are pasted in layers until a solid-appearing hill is formed, the whole being painted in appropriate colours when dry. Wonderful hills can be turned out like this but few model soldiers will stand up on them. It is possible to make these hills and then mould sheets of thin plasticine over them, conforming to the contours of the hills, thus making a very excellent hill and without using a great deal of plasticine.

When one commences war games it is often found that terrain assumes an almost 'symbolic' appearance in that the hills are stepped affairs of decreasing-sized pieces of wood being placed one upon the other. These are very good from the point of view of standing figures upon them but hardly realistic in appearance. In Wells's book *Little Wars* this type of hill is featured prominently in almost every photograph.

There is another method of making hills but again not too successful from the point of view of keeping figures erect upon it. This consists of a large cloth of green baize or felt which is stretched over the table, and hills are made by placing books, pieces of wood, etc., under the cloth, thus causing a humped effect.

There are so many admirable types of scenery available from model-railway firms that it is almost a waste of time to make one's own. Trees can be purchased in plastic that look very real and are quite cheap. They can also be made from loofah sponge or foam plastic dyed green and stuck on to pieces of twig, or there is a type of lichen moss available that makes wonderful trees. When war games started in the writer's house, trees were made plentifully from pine-cones dyed green and fixed to the table with a daub of plasticine!

There are model-railway kits that provide, at very reasonable prices, such accessories as stone walls, rail fencing, corn-stooks, hedges and the like; or the purist can make them quite adequately. The stone walls can be strips of balsa wood or any other similar material covered with the brickwork paper also obtainable at model-railway shops. The fencing can be made of wire and wood uprights, the hedges of foam plastic or loofah sponge and the corn-stooks from either plasticine or plaster of Paris suitably painted. Bridges can be made from balsa wood and covered with brick or stonework paper. There is great scope for originality when making bridges, which can be of any type, from the trestle bridge beloved of American Civil War and Western films to the crumbling stone bridge such as one encounters on Dartmoor.

Houses also make interesting models—they can either be made from scratch, made up from the numerous plastic kits on the market, or purchased ready-made. The home-made house can, again, be of many types and may be whole or half destroyed, according to the whim of the model-maker. The many plastic kits that turn out houses have the disadvantage of usually being modern abodes that do not always fit in with the period in which the war gamer is fighting, but Airfix turn out timbered residences that can quite easily be painted up in 'period' fashion. Triang make some very realistic houses out of a type of rubber or plastic. They come in a good variety and are not particularly expensive. It is possible to obtain churches, barns, cottages, shops, terraced houses, oast-houses and other types, many of which fit in perfectly with terrain representing the past hundred years or so.

One feature to be considered when dealing with houses lies in whether or not the war gamer in fact wishes to station men inside them during a battle. In the experience of the writer, this rarely works out well, as the player crams hordes of men unrealistically into the houses and then argues about who can actually poke his rifle from a window or door and really be counted as firing! In order that a house or a village makes its correct contribution to the aims and objectives of a war game, it is necessary that soldiers should be able to take cover in it, but it is considered best if this is done in 'token' fashion. In other words, houses are rated according to their size, and marked for five or ten men as the case may be. Those men are then taken off the battlefield and kept separately. They are counted for firing and mêlée purposes as being within the houses (subject to conditions laid down in the rules given further on in the book) and are removed from their separate positions and placed amongst the casualties.

A feature that gives a final polish to the appearance of the war-games table and, at the same time, plays an important part in the actual game itself, is suitable background scenery. Model-railway enthusiasts use sheets of suitably printed scenic effects stuck on to vertical surfaces behind their hills, bridges and railway track, thus giving a pleasing and realistic finish to their layout. War gamers can utilize this equipment to aid in giving battles realism in the following manner—take enough of this scenic strip to extend along the whole of both baselines of the war-games table (and the sides if desired), stick it to thick cardboard or to plywood and cut it to shape so that the hills, trees, etc., form an irregular horizon. Make these lengths of scenery about 18 inches long so that they can be fixed along your baseline to leave small gaps between each piece. Tack the lengths of scenery on to a length of 2 in. × 1 in. wood so that it will stand up, giving erect scenery behind which is a 2-inch-wide shelf. This length of timber is fixed along the baseline of your table.

When a terrain is laid extend your roads up to the baseline and continue them via the scenic background by leaving gaps between scenery at the points at which the roads end on the table; the same thing can be done with rivers. There will thus be formed gaps or defiles through which the roads run off the table, and it is through these defiles that troops must enter and leave the table. Thus, when the battle is commencing, the troops can enter only along the defined roads; reinforcements can be kept behind the scenery, out of sight of your opponent, and brought on the table via the gaps when required. Retreating forces must, in the same way, leave the table by the roads running through the gaps. This gives added interest to a fighting retreat, as the army falling back has to keep open its line of retreat whilst the victorious forces are trying hard to cut that same avenue of escape.

To conclude, laying out terrain can be made as complicated as desired or as simple as to be laid in a few seconds. It is always a large part of the fun of war gaming to be able to lay out an interesting terrain and then, after fighting over it, to see if the various features you have constructed have played their part and given an exciting battle. A good terrain is not necessarily a cluttered one. Some of the best battles take place on the bare table with merely a hill, clump of trees, one house and a stone wall. Experience will aid the war gamer in this field and he will eventually become a connoisseur, able to detect the phoney terrain from the good one at a glance, but always able to lay out his troops so that he takes the fullest advantage of the salient features of the war-games table and deploys his forces accordingly.

4

Organizing a Campaign

WHEN one first begins to play at war games, or, to put the matter in a more technical light, when one begins to fight battles, satisfaction is obtained at the conclusion of a single battle. In this fight one side wins and the other force, with perhaps less grace, loses—the battle ends and it is finished, having no connection with any other similar affray or with any battle that is to come. Such a course soon palls and the players discover an urge to relate this victory or defeat to the conditions applying in the next battle, the casualties incurred having some effect on the conflict in which that army next fought. In other words, the war gamers have got the urge to formulate rules and conditions governing a campaign as opposed to a single, individual battle. Campaigns on the war-games table are sometimes complicated affairs, with their problems of casualties, attrition, lines of communication, sieges, reinforcements and the like. The issue of the battle is conditional upon the battle that went before, to a certain extent, and the battle that is being fought will have a similar effect upon the battle that is to come—strategy has to be practised equally with tactics.

In the first instance, the players must settle upon the campaign they wish to fight. In this they are governed to some extent by the type of soldiers they possess—it is a trifle unconventional to fight the Waterloo campaign if one has only troops of the American Civil War! If it is decided to re-fight an actual campaign of history then it is relatively easy—the first requirement is a map of the territory over which the war was fought, next accumulate all possible information of the troops of the opposing sides, scale down those numbers to suit available soldiers and commence map moves.

On the other hand, a completely mythical campaign is often conducted, using fancifully uniformed troops of imaginary countries and with highly coloured reasons for fighting the war. This can be fascinating, as ruling houses, petty dukedoms, jealous heirs and dashing princes provide unlimited excuses for one state declaring war on another adjacent dukedom, or for those gaily coloured Hussars to be sent to the distant frontier where they will die gallantly fighting off the hordes of savage tribesmen threatening their country.

Whatever the type of campaign, the first essential is a master-map—this is a large map of the entire war area which is divided into squares for easy calculation of movement—each side moving one square per map move. The rate of movement must be so worked out as to cope with the rates of movement of the various types of troops: thus infantry move perhaps one mile per move, whilst cavalry move two and so on. Moves on roads are further than across country and transport can move only by road. Decide if both players move their map forces simultaneously or in turn, deciding by dice throw the order of move so that one player does not move first continuously. Indicate position of forces by using coloured pins or flags to denote the various forces that are moving. It is a sound idea to relate the rates of movement on the map with those applying on the war-games table, thus make each move on the map an inch, whilst an inch also represents a full game move on the table. In this way it is possible to assess distances necessary to be covered by a reinforcing army, thus they may be 5 inches away from the battle on the map, which means that they will arrive on the table after five game moves.

When a contact is made upon the map, the terrain is reproduced on the war-games table; unless the map used is of a very large scale it is difficult to reproduce accurately the terrain which often has to be rigged in an interesting fashion. The obvious features of the map are made up, thus a road would move in the direction indicated on the map, as would a river. If there is a crossroads in the centre of the map square then it is shown in the centre of the war-games table. But, other than those obvious salient features, the rest of the terrain should be made in such a fashion that both sides get a 'fair crack of the whip'—hills are reasonably evenly distributed, villages are made accessible to both sides, and generally one can say that one terrain feature of an advantageous nature on this side of the table is balanced by another piece of roughly the same benefit on the other. This makes for an even and interesting battle, except in cases where one side has to prepare its own defensive position, for example, where terrain can be erected definitely to the advantage of that side.

Imaginative players can work out innumerable situations and rules to cover the use of maps, but a general set of rules and conditions are suggested at the end of this chapter. To give the right air of continuity it is important that the map campaign shows objectives, because one of the saddest omissions in war games often is the lack of objectives which cause games to end in stalemate or argument. Both sides must establish headquarters or points of supply with which they must keep in contact. This automatically means that lines of communication are formed which have to be guarded by their owners and attempted to be cut by the enemy. If one gets across the lines of communication of the enemy then that enemy cannot make any forward moves for his troops being supplied by this route, and for each move made after the actual cutting of the line some sort of penalty must be bestowed.

Casualties from one battle must be considered to have an effect on future strengths of one's army—one system could be based upon the saving-throw method in which one throws a dice to determine which hits are killed and removed from the table and which are only wounded. If *both* killed and wounded were removed but a note taken of the relative figures, so that in the next battle those only wounded were allowed to take part in that contest whilst the killed were out for good—then an elementary system of attrition has been established. Another method is to divide all casualties after a battle into three—one-third are dead, one-third severely wounded and one-third slightly wounded. The dead, oddly enough, go to the Recruit

Intake, the severely wounded go to the Base Hospital and the slightly wounded go to the Field Hospital. Before the next battle is fought the following has to be worked out—the men in the Recruit Intake are scheduled to return to the army for the third battle following the one about to be fought, the severely wounded in the Base Hospital can return for the second battle to be fought, whilst the slightly wounded are ready and available for the battle about to take place. This might sound very complicated, but it is easily handled if a battle diary is made out, divided into horizontal sections each one labelled 'Game Move No. 1, Game Move No. 2' and so on, so that it is possible to enter that the first battle began on Game Move 1 and ended on Game Move 8. Map moves took up the next four moves, then the second battle commenced on Game Move 12, etc. In this way a complete chronological record of the campaign is held by each player. Another good method of final assessment is shown at the end of the Rules for Modern Warfare (after Lionel Tarr).

One departure from realism that is difficult to counter lies in the fact that, in real life, units moving across country would have their movements largely concealed from each other unless scouting patrols discovered them. On the map it is hard for two players to reproduce this surprise element without getting highly involved. War gamers Warwick Hale and Peter Pringle of Chatham have worked out a simple but highly effective means of reproducing hidden troop movements—which they use most successfully. When they select their master-map to cover the area over which the campaign is to be fought, they divide it into squares of one inch, each square being formed by the gridded lines running horizontally and vertically over the map. Each of these grid lines is given a number if it is a line running horizontally and a letter if it runs vertically—thus a square in the immediate left-hand top corner would be 'A1'. They then collect a large number of empty matchboxes, one for each map square, which they glue together by their tops and bottoms so that a large 'box' is formed with the matchbox trays opening on either side. Each tray is labelled with its respective letter and number, thus 'A1', 'B1' and so on. Each separate force is written down on a small piece of card, and as that force moves over the map it is placed in the matchbox representing the map square in which the force lies at that moment. When each side finds that a matchbox has got two pieces of card inside, one belonging to each army, then those two sides are deemed to have made a 'contact' in the square in question. That square is then topographically reproduced on the war-games table and the battle takes place. Obviously, there are many other types of tactics for which these boxes can be used, including retreats, lines of communication, cavalry scouting patrols, etc., etc.

An advanced and not too easy method of using maps for a campaign was tried in Southampton recently during an attempt to re-fight the Franco-Prussian War. In this campaign maps of the actual battlefields of that war were used, such as Worth Gravelotte, Mars-la-Tour, etc. Each force was given a base. The French had Châlons and the Prussians had Mannheim and the battlefield on which the first battle of the campaign took place was deemed to be fifty game moves from that base. Thus, if the Prussians won and forced the French back on to the next scheduled battlefield, the French had got a certain number of moves nearer to their own base whilst the Prussians had moved that same number further away from their base. The importance of this lay in the fact that each regiment on each side had a second or reserve battalion at Base when the campaign started and these reserve units were considered to be moving forward towards their main armies at a certain stated rate of map movement from the moment the campaign started. Thus, depleted forces could be brought up to strength by the arrival of these reserves so that a retreating army would be reinforced sooner than the advancing army, which would give it a chance to halt the retreat and prolong the campaign.

Each battle of the campaign was fought in *three* parts, with the battlefield divided into three equal sections, in each of which one corps fought against the same number of the enemy (subject to some conditions mentioned later), so that the French Army consisted of a centre corps, and a right-flank corps, and a left-flank corps—the Prussians being organized in the same

D

fashion. The winner of two out of three of these part-battles had won the whole battle. Thus it might be that the French won the battle on the right flank, but their centre and left flanks were beaten, thus they had lost the whole battle. The loser retreated to the next designated battlefield or by taking one of the alternative courses permitted in the following rules:

The map for each battle consisted of *nine* squares (each 6 in. × 6 in.). Thus they corresponded on the scale of 1 inch equalled 1 foot to the actual war-games table, which was 6 ft. × 6 ft.—and a map move of 1 inch equalled a troop movement of 1 foot on the table. The actual battle was fought in the three horizontal middle squares. One side nominated which of the three battle squares they intended to use for their first battle, *but* both sides laid down *on the map* their *entire* forces in all three squares—this did not have to be revealed to each other, thus giving a certain element of surprise as to formation of army.

At the start of the battle, or at any time during the battle, one commander could declare that any specific units were moving from other squares into battle square (to be moved on the map at the decided scale of speed). Once a unit enters the battle square they are lost to the force they have just left for that *entire* set of three battles.

From each battle square, passing through the map squares behind and in front, roads are marked which lead to the next scheduled battlefield. Thus sets of each nine battlefield squares are related to one another by this system of roads. The loser of a battle may do one of the following:

1. He may retreat his forces off each of the three squares of the battlefield on which he has just lost, via the necessary roads, to the next designated battlefield.

2. If the defeated commander feels that the situation demands it, he may move a defeated *corps* from one battle square into any one of the three squares behind, thus he might be able to cover the retreat of one or both of his other corps. If he does this, a battle takes place in this new square with both sides

being permitted to lay down their troops within 6 inches of the centre line (or curtain). Each side will lose laid-down percentages of casualties from first battle before second battle begins (usually 25 per cent. of their total casualties).

If the winning force manages to get a force of not less than one cavalry regiment in strength *across* the road leading to the next battlefield, then the retreating commander has the following alternatives:

(a) He may attempt to retreat along another road to the scheduled battlefield, which may mean separation from his other allied forces for the next three-square battle series (which would mean that two 'A' corps faced three 'B' corps on three battlefields, with one corps spare and available to move into actual battle square as reinforcements).

(b) He may fight his way through Intercepting Force. In this case, the Retreating Force throw dice (saving throw of 5 or 6) for *the same number of men as there are in the intercepting force PLUS* one man for each man of the Interceptors' force, who may be within one cavalry move of the Interceptors' commander. The Intercepting Force throw dice for *half* their number. Thus if the Intercepting Force consisted of 20 cavalry (counting as 2 points each) with another 60 infantry of their own side 9 inches away, then the retreating force would throw for 40 points to begin with (40 infantry or 20 cavalry) *plus* another 60 points to cover the supporting troops. The Interceptors would only throw for *10* cavalry.

Having done this, the remainder of the Retreating Force are deemed to have broken through *unless* Interceptors' strength plus supporting troops equals or exceeds the number of the retreating force. Any retreating force that has had to fight its way through to its new battlefield will, on arrival, be considered to be fatigued and will move only half-distance moves for the first two game moves.

It is pointed out, to further complicate matters, that the situations mentioned in the preceding paragraphs, which concern the interception of a retreating force, under certain appropriate conditions may have to take place either on the actual war-games table, or may be performed as map moves and decided on paper without actually moving troops.

GENERAL RULES FOR MAP MOVEMENT

1. Where possible, maps will be scaled to war-games table, thus if table is 6 ft. × 6 ft. map could well be 6 in. × 6 in. In this case, a 6-inch move on the actual table (normal single infantry move) would be represented on the map by a half-inch move. This facilitates working out distance from actual point of contact of other forces marked on map.

2. If the map is of a smaller scale, then it could be scaled so that one inch equals one mile—this usually applies in the case of printed maps. When this scale is in use, the following rate of movement on the map is advised:

Infantry on road	1 in. per game move
Cavalry „	1½ in. „
Infantry across country	½ in. „
Cavalry „	1 in. „
Field artillery	As infantry
Horse artillery	As cavalry
Night map moves	Half above distances.

3. Rivers can be crossed only where there are bridges or fords, when it takes them one complete move to cross (if crossing is unopposed).

4. Roads and rivers can be used only by one regiment abreast, thus an army will stretch along road relative to the number of units of which it is composed.

5. Mountains can be crossed only where roads are shown to lead over them.

6. An army which has remained in one position for two map moves is considered to be in a prepared position and, if

attacked, its commander may draw his own battle map (but must include salient features such as rivers, roads, etc.). If both flanks rest on unturnable obstacles—which can be done only if such obstacles appear on the main map—then the army in position lays down up to the half-way mark on the war-games table whilst the attacker deploys on the baseline after the defender has completed his layout. If the flanks are not secured then the attacker can, if his map move allows, make a flank approach. The defender must at the outset have written down on his map the precise disposition of his troops. The attacker now writes down his dispositions. Both generals now throw the dice three times each. If the attacker wins two throws, then the defender must lay down his troops in strict accordance with his written map dispositions, whilst the attacker can lay down on the flanking baseline and launch his attack against the defender's flank. If the defender wins two throws, then he can change his dispositions from front to flank to meet the attack; in this case the battle is fought up and down the table instead of across it. If the defender wins all three throws, then, instead of changing front, he can attack the enemy as they march across his front. The attacker will lay out in order of march according to his written dispositions, thus presenting his own flank to the counter-attack.

7. Map moves can be made simultaneously by both players on their own maps *or* they can be made in turn (dice being thrown for order) on the single master-map. They can also be made continuous moves, so that a player can advance his army along a road, checking every six or so moves to ascertain if a contact would have been made with the enemy. If this is the case, then the moves are traced back to the point where the contact was made and the battle is then deemed to have been forced there—arrangements following in the usual way to fight said battle.

8. Lines of communication can be marked and, if cut, the general in question has so many moves to reopen them, capture a town and thus replenish his supplies. If he does neither, then that general loses a percentage number of his troops for each

succeeding move in which the lines remain cut. There are so many different methods to be followed in such cases and so many theories and ideas around that this rule has purposely been left in rather a vague state!

9. When map moves are made alternately, certain situations present themselves. For instance, if the army moving *second* makes a contact after the first army has moved, it must be decided whether the first moving army was advancing or retreating. If it was advancing, then presumably contact would be made between opposing advance guards. This is simulated by both commanders making out an order of march, dividing their armies into advanced guard, centre and rearguard, and allowing one map move between each body (equals one game move on the table). Thus it is possible to get a realistic situation of cavalry advance guards fighting for possession of ground on which their main bodies wish later to deploy.

If the first moving army was retreating before the enemy, then the same situation in reverse applies. The commander of the army being attacked could decide whether to leave his rearguard to fight a delaying action or to commit his whole army. Here the terrain would enter into the picture. It must be decided (by dice usually) which of the two generals lays out the terrain so that, if the retreating general were laying it, he could make a terrain offering a chance of a delaying action, for example.

Terrain also must be considered when one attempts any form of pursuit after a battle. This can be covered by a system in which a number of adjoining map squares are drawn so that the surrounding country is known. It must also be considered whether the retreating army is moving off in good order or if they are routed. This could be related to the number of units still in fighting shape and the damage done to the opposing army. If an army is routed pursuit will simply be a continuation of the battle, the routed army will be flying in disorder hotly pursued by the victor's cavalry. Length of pursuit would be related to the number of moves remaining of the actual battle day plus the following night. Thus a battle that has taken five game moves has three day moves left plus four night moves (at half-rate).

During the pursuit, the victor would count the points total of his pursuers (cavalry 2 pts., infantry 1 pt.), and for every 5 points he throws one dice, half the score of which counts as enemy casualties who have to be thrown for with a 5 or 6 to save them. The pursuing force would move across the map as far as they actually pursued, in addition to any advance made during the battle.

If the beaten army retires in good order then it must be formed up in column of march. The victor, provided he has suitable cavalry force remaining, may start out one map move later, his infantry following three moves later.

It is possible to carry on for a very long time with intriguing variations of map rules covering most of the facets of actual warfare. The enthusiastic war gamer will readily be able to formulate his own ideas and rules, based perhaps on what has been written here. The difference between war games in which maps are used and those fought singly and without maps are the differences between a man and a boy!

It should be pointed out that many of the rules and suggestions contained in this chapter are from the agile brain of the author's most frequent opponent—Tony Bath. They have been worked out by him and used in games and campaigns fought between us over the last few years—they don't all work out successfully but in every case it has to be admitted that a considerable amount of ingenuity and brainwork has gone into their formulation.

5

How to Start a War Game

ALL the rules contained in this book begin with the actual events
that take place on the war-games table, i.e. the move, firing,
then hand-to-hand fighting, etc. But before troops can be
moved or can fire they have to be laid out on the table—arranged
or deployed for battle as it were—and there are a number of
different ways in which this can be carried out.

In the first place it is a great time-saver to draw maps of
the actual table, to a rough scale if desired (say 1 inch on the
map/diagram to 1 foot of the table). The map is sent to one's
opponent a few days before the battle is to be fought, and in
this way both players have a chance to study the terrain, to
make their plans, decide where they wish to deploy their force
and work out their line of attack or defence, as the case may be.
Thus, on the day of battle, when the visiting general arrives,
the 'home' player has set out the terrain in accordance with the
map and the battlefield is ready.

The next thing to be decided is what type of battle it is to be
—a set-piece battle, an encounter battle, a battle for a prepared
position, etc. This is done by considering the factors leading up
to the battle, if one is fighting a campaign in which earlier troop
movements have been done on maps, or by deciding the time
of day at which the opposing forces met. Before commencing
the battle, throw a single dice—1: 6 a.m.; 2: 9 a.m.; 3: 1 p.m.;
4: 4 p.m.; 5: 7 p.m.; 6: 9 p.m. Presuming that daylight lasts
for 15 hours (from 6 a.m. until 9 p.m.) a day will last for ten
game moves, each game move representing 1½ hours. The
battle will take the relevant number of moves according to the

time at which it began. Thus a battle beginning at 1 p.m. will last five game moves when nightfall will take place. Nightfall lasts four game moves, during which time opposing forces may re-group and move the appropriate distance possible in four moves. A curtain should be placed between the armies so that they may make their night moves unseen by each other, otherwise the moves should be written down and then made simultaneously.

If a battle commences at or before 1 p.m. it is considered to be an encounter battle, a situation in which the advance forces of two armies meet, possibly accidentally, as at Gettysburg, and a battle is precipitated. In this case both players lay down their forces in any desired formation along their baselines and a curtain is drawn across the table between them as they assemble, thus giving some element of surprise.

A battle that begins at 4 p.m. (i.e. with three moves to go before nightfall) means that both sides again lay down on the baselines and use the three moves to gain possession of ground they wish to hold for the following day's battle. If this brings opposing units into contact or firing range then fighting will take place. At the end of the three moves the curtain will be replaced and the armies re-group, but the troops cannot be moved beyond the front line established at nightfall.

When the battle is such that troops are laid out on the baselines, much time can be saved by laying down 'representative' units—put out only two men of each unit, placed so as to show the area over which the unit is deployed, move these representative forces instead of laying out full units, until actual contact is made by fire or mêlée when the full units are placed on the table. Another method, possibly better, is to make movement trays by covering a piece of card with a thin layer of plasticine, or by glueing on to the piece of card some slots into which the bases of troops can be fitted; they will also adhere to the plasticine if that is the method used. These cards should be of a size so that they represent the area that the unit would cover when in double rank if the card is placed horizontally, and the area covered when the unit is in column if the card is placed vertically. On each card fit two men as before, one at each end of the card, and perhaps an officer or standard bearer in the middle of the card to add colour! By moving these representative units during the opening moves of a battle a great deal of time is saved that can later be usefully spent on actual fighting.

If the contact between the two forces is made on or after 7 p.m. then no fighting takes place on that day, it is considered that the units have approached each other towards the end of the day, have sized each other up and deployed into battle formation during the night so that the battle can commence at daybreak. To simulate this situation, both armies are allowed to form up on their entire half of the table, with the curtain drawn between them. When both players are ready the curtain is raised and both armies are found, if desired, to be laid down right up to the curtain. Thus, battle takes place almost at once as opposing forces are within range of each other. This type of game provides hectic fighting from the word 'go' and is ideal when there is a time limit for playing and as much action as possible is required.

There are other alternative methods of beginning battles. These can really come under the heading of war games that are fought both on maps and on the table. It is possible, when carrying out a map campaign, to simulate situations in which delaying actions are fought, in which troops in prepared positions fight off their attackers, smaller forces fighting to hold a defile or bridge against larger numbers, and other inter-esting situations.

It is difficult in war games to work out a situation in which a smaller force has a chance to fight with any success against a larger force, or where undisciplined native troops fight against organized armies. The first situation is one that occurs fre-quently in real life and, in map campaigns, often crops up—the resulting battle usually being quickly over and little fun for either contestant. One method of handling the situation is to permit the smaller force to have a terrain specifically suited to it, so that it is in a very well-prepared defensive position (it can even be a terrain planned and laid out by the player handling the weaker side). Possibly the 'rigging' of the terrain holds the greatest opportunities for situations involving small and larger forces, because other factors can be introduced, such as defiles or bridges held by a force and against which the larger army can deploy only part of its numbers, or a front in which the small force works on interior lines so that it can swiftly move men from one flank to the other whilst the larger force has to work on a bigger basis. A front that narrows so that only fairly equal forces can meet is another angle, or a terrain divided into two by an almost uncrossable river or mountain range, so that the larger force has to decide in which half of the table he will mass, whilst the smaller force needs to be only in one half, possibly against half the enemy forces, which will give him parity.

It must be confessed that the question of how to fight a successful action with natives against disciplined troops has yet to be completely solved by the writer. One method allows the natives to move a longer distance than the troops, or to time the moves and have the disciplined troops on movement trays so that they can move as one whilst the natives move individually in a rabble. Another means lies in having low morale ratings for natives when the situation arises that the morale of both or either side is in question. A compromise can lie in having very much larger numbers of natives with low firepower against well-armed disciplined troops in smaller numbers and possibly with a Gatling gun or a mountain howitzer.

An interesting innovation frequently used by the writer is to give both players the chance to select their own force, give each infantryman a points value of 1, cavalry 2 and a gun 10 points. Then lay down that each army can consist of 250 points; both players are able to study the terrain, pick the side from which they wish to fight and then select the army that they feel will best handle that type of terrain and their planned battle. A rigged battle with a definite objective that has to be held or carried within, say, three hours—the force having most men in or around the village, or the force that manages to have the most men adjacent to their opponents' baseline by 10 p.m.—or both players declare the site of their army headquarters and the objective of the game is to overrun that HQ, when the force concerned must make a fighting retreat off the table.

It is always interesting to have a battle in which one or both players have reinforcements arriving at some stage—this is easily worked by saying that the reinforcements will arrive on their own armies' baseline at the end of the fourth game move, for example; or to have moves on the map that conclude with a contact between opposing forces, when all forces in the vicinity move hurriedly towards the battle to reinforce their comrades, the map moves being scaled to the game moves at, for example, one map mile equals one game move, so that one measures on the map and finds that he has a force of cavalry five miles from the battle area—thus that force will arrive on their nearest flank or position at the end of the fifth game move. It can be previously arranged that the forces in the actual battle total 250 points, whilst any reinforcements that are to arrive must not total more than another 100 points—in this manner a situation is avoided where one army becomes faced with overwhelming numbers and the game declines into a walkover.

6

Ancient Warfare

RULES* AND DEMONSTRATION BATTLE: 'THE BATTLE OF TRIMSOS'

THE MOVE

1. Before each move both players throw dice, highest scorer moves first. Second mover fires first.

2. Moves are as follows:

Heavy Infantry	6 inches
medium "	7·5 "
Light Infantry	9 "
Heavy Cavalry	12 "
Light Cavalry	15 "
Chariots	15 "
Elephants	12 "
War Engines on Wheels	6 "
Supply Carts	12 "

When moving by road, all arms add 3 inches to their move.

3. Moving uphill, through woods or over marshland: Light troops move full distance. Heavy troops move half distance (except in case of hills unoccupied by enemy when normal distance can be moved).

* These rules are those devised and used by Tony Bath—they also owe a debt to Mr G. Bantock and Archie Cass.

4. All units are considered to be able to increase their speed (i.e. running) occasionally—this is represented by permitting troops to move double distance *every other move* if desired. Light troops cannot fire when they have moved double distance. To show which units have moved double, at the conclusion of the move place a coloured counter against that unit, thus indicating that they cannot fire nor move double distance again next move.

5. Double moves are never permitted when climbing hills, descending hills, moving through woods or crossing marshland or rivers.

6. Rivers, unless specifically stated to be uncrossable except at bridges or fords, can be classified as under:

Class A river. A unit takes 6 inches to cross this river and cannot fire during this move.

Class B river. A unit takes 3 inches to cross this river and may fire whilst so doing.

7. To cross a wall, hedge or fence takes 3 inches of the move.

8. Staff officers may move up to 24 inches each move.

9. All units must be led by their officers during an advance, thus if a unit remains stationary its officers and standard bearers can be placed in rear and out of the field of fire.

MISSILE FIRE

1. When moving has been carried out by both sides (except in case of 'split move' by horse archers, explained later) then firing takes place, player who moved second fires first.

2. *Ranges:* Longbow, crossbow or sling

> Long Range is   24 inches
> Medium   12   ,,
> Close   6   ,,

Javelin and spearmen
> Long Range is   9 inches

Medium	6 inches
Close	3 ,,

Pilum of Romans
Close Range only 3 ,,

War Engines: heavy stone thrower
Long Range is   24 inches

Medium	12 ,,
Close	6 ,,

War Engines: light stone thrower
Ranges as heavy stone thrower.

3. *Method of firing*. All missile men are deemed to fire in volleys consisting of five men, thus twenty men would fire four volleys, for example. For each volley one dice is thrown and casualties are computed as below:

At long range deduct *three* from each dice score

At medium range ,, *two*   ,,

At short range   ,, *one*   ,,

The number remaining after deduction is the total of hits scored on the enemy, thus a dice showing 5 at long range would score two hits.

Any troops left over after divided up into volleys of five men may be fired as individuals in the following manner:

At long range must throw a *six* on the dice to hit

At medium range   ,,   *five or six*   ,,

At close range   ,,   *four, five or six* ,,

War Engines: Before discovering how many hits are scored, a dice must be thrown to see if the engine is loaded. Thus if the dice shows *four*, *five* or *six* it is loaded and may fire, but if *one*, *two* or *three* is shown then it is not loaded and may not fire that move.

Heavy stone throwers firing at 24-inch range must throw a *six* to score a hit, at 12-inch range a *five* or *six* and at 6-inch range a *four, five* or *six*. All men within a 4-inch radius of the point where the stone dropped are killed.

Light stone thrower requires the same scores to hit but only kills men within a 2-inch radius of hit.

4. If the troops fired upon are under cover (i.e. behind a wall, in the edges of a wood or in a house) then a further *one* is deducted from the dice throws as shown above.

5. Mounted bowmen may, on alternate moves, take a double move and move only part of the distance, then fire, and move back the remainder of their move distance (out of range if required). This is known as a 'split move' and takes place actually during the move and not at the conclusion as does other firing. Even if the mounted archers eventually complete this split move, so that they are out of range of the troops upon whom they have fired, those troops may earn the right to fire upon the mounted archers in the normal way and at the closest range at which the archers attained. This right to fire back is earned by throwing a dice and scoring *four*, *five* or *six*.

6. In all cases and whatsoever formation a unit may be in, only the first *two* ranks may fire. The sole exception lies in ranks other than the first two being upon a height or higher elevation so that they can fire over their first two ranks.

7. War Engines must have a crew of at least three men.

8. Angle of fire for all missiles is 50 degrees to right or left of facing position.

9. A War Engine when fired upon by another War Engine can be knocked out permanently if the firer is of a larger size than the victim. If hit by one of its own size it is out of action for the next two moves. If hit by one of smaller size it is out of action for one move.

DECIDING CASUALTIES

To lessen the speed at which troops are killed and removed from the game, and also to encourage aggressive tactics, the following formula has been devised to determine which of the casualties are killed and out permanently or only wounded and able to carry on. This method can be used with casualties from both missile fire and from mêlées.

If, for example, ten men have been hit—take eight white dice and two coloured dice (the white representing other ranks and the coloured officers)—coloured dice are used in the proportion of one coloured dice to every five casualties thus determining whether or not officers have been hit. Throw the dice in one throw and compute casualties by the following scale:

If the soldier is unarmoured and has no shield he must throw a *six* to survive.

Armour or shield: 5 or 6.

Armour and shield: 4, 5 or 6.

Unarmoured cavalry: 5. 6 saves rider alone.

Armoured cavalry: 5 or 6. 4 saves rider alone.

Fully mailed cavalry: 4, 5 or 6. 3 saves rider alone.

Casualties from pilum or crossbow must throw a *six* however clad, provided the hit is at close range.

HAND-TO-HAND FIGHTING

A mêlée or hand-to-hand combat is formed when one body of troops is brought into direct contact with another similar body, the attacker then declaring that he has forced a mêlée. Fighting takes place and casualties are determined subject to the following conditions:

1. Whatever formation the opposing forces may assume, the fighting only takes place between the *two* front ranks of each unit. It consists of two rounds of fighting per move, in the second round gaps in the front ranks may be made up from men brought forward from the unit's second rank.

2. The procedure is as follows: Force A moves into contact with Force B (Force A being 20 cavalrymen, Force B being 30 infantrymen). As cavalrymen count 2 points and infantrymen

E

count 1 point, the front rank of Force A consisting of 10 cavalrymen (second rank formed by remaining 10) counts as 20 points. Force B is lined up with 15 men in each rank— so that Force B counts 15 points for the first round of fighting.

One dice is thrown for every *five* points involved, so that Force A have four dice and Force B have three dice.

An attacking force is deemed to have a certain 'shock' value known as impetus—which means that *for the first round of fighting only* Force A can add *one* to each of their dice totals.

Let us assume that Force A throw their four dice and score 5, 4, 3 and 2, which, with *one* added to each dice, gives them a total of 18. Force B throw their three dice and score 6, 6 and 4—a total of 16. Force A have therefore caused casualties to Force B of *nine* points whilst Force B have caused casualties to Force A of *eight* points. The total casualties are determined by counting *half* the total dice scored as casualties.

In the case of this particular mêlée, Force A would lose 4 cavalrymen (worth 2 points each) whilst Force B would lose 9 infantrymen.

For the second round of fighting Force A would be able to reinforce their front line up to the same strength, whilst Force B would be able to do the same—so the same routine would take place again. Casualties having been determined and removed, both forces now have to discover how their *morale* stands after this encounter (see Morale Section, p. 69). This morale rating is subject to certain factors such as one unit losing all its officers, one unit being in overwhelming strength, etc. Should both sides' morale rating enable them to stay in their present positions, further rounds of fighting take place at the conclusion of the next move; this carries on until one unit is forced to withdraw because of low morale or insufficient numbers to continue the fight.

It is pointed out that in describing this hypothetical mêlée no account has been taken of the effect on casualties of using the 'saving' dice throws mentioned earlier.

All mêlées are subject to various conditions as outlined herewith:

1. *Impetus bonus*. As already explained, this is a bonus of *one* added to each dice score thrown by attacking force on the *first* round of hand-to-hand fighting. It is given under the following conditions:

(a) Troops charging uphill or at defences such as walls, fences, houses, etc., do *not* get impetus bonus.

(b) Troops charging downhill get *double* impetus bonus.

(c) Troops charging across a river do *not* get impetus bonus.

2. *Cavalry attacking spearmen* in double rank require dice throw of 4, 5 or 6 to charge home. If spearmen in three ranks, then cavalry require 5 or 6 to charge home. If cavalry fail to charge home (i.e. by throwing less than totals required) then a second dice is thrown and if 1, 2 or 3 is thrown the cavalry swerve to their right, 4, 5 or 6 means they swerve to their left. They actually swerve a distance far enough to make up their full move—so that if they have moved a double move to attack the infantry and used only 16 inches of it to reach the formed-up infantry, then their swerving distance will be a further 8 inches which will make up their entitled distance of 24 inches.

3. *Infantry behind defences* deprive attackers of their impetus bonus, they also add *one* to their morale throw at end of mêlée and *one* to their saving throw if used.

4. *Officers*. If either side loses all its officers after one round of fighting it must throw dice to see how its morale stands (see Morale Section). If one or both sides have no officers left at end of mêlée second round then both officerless forces throw for their morale as per section in Morale.

5. *Overwhelming numbers*. If a force is outnumbered 2 to 1 by similar troops or by cavalry, 3 to 1 light troops against heavy, 4 to 1 infantry against cavalry (rear ranks not actively engaged can be counted for this purpose), then only *one* round of fighting takes place, after which weaker force must throw for their morale as per appropriate section in Morale.

6. *Superior numbers*. If a situation arises where one side has obviously superior numbers in mêlée (for example, in case

where weaker side has beaten morale throw of dice, although facing overwhelming numbers) then any man facing two of the enemy must try to dodge fighting against both of them—this he can do by throwing 5 or 6 on the dice if he is an infantryman or 4, 5 or 6 if he is a cavalryman. If he is unable to dodge, then he throws only one dice in individual combat against the enemy's $1\frac{1}{2}$ dice (highest total score wins).

7. *Flank or rear attacks*. If a unit is able to be attacked on its flank or rear and has no men facing in that particular direction to avoid such a situation, then the attackers have a definite advantage which can be countered only by the force being attacked throwing one dice and acting in accordance with appropriate scale laid down in Morale Section.

8. *Firing*. Attacked troops who can fire will always do so, and attackers moving in to attack must take fire from *all* units whose line of fire they cross.

The troops under attack have to decide at what range they may fire on their attackers—for example, if the attackers move 12 inches to make the attack then the defenders throw a dice, and if they score 1, 2 or 3 then they fire at 12-inch range, if they fire at 6-inch range then they must have thrown 4, 5 or 6.

Provided that they have not moved a double move in coming in to attack, the attackers may also fire on the defenders (provided that they are missile men). In the same way as in the last paragraph they throw a dice to see at what range they fire on the defenders.

Supporting fire may be given during an attack, i.e. if Force A's infantry attack a unit of Force B, then other missile troops of Force A in the vicinity may fire on the unit being attacked as Force A's infantry go in—firing being done at normal ranges only. The firing either takes place over the heads of the attackers or across their front as they go in.

9. *Reinforcing mêlée*. If Force A moves first and attacks Force B, then it is quite fair for Force B to move reinforcing troops from adjacent positions into the mêlée—these troops will get the advantage of impetus bonus if applicable.

Troops reinforcing a mêlée that has already been going on

for one or more moves do *not* get impetus bonus, nor can they claim a flank or rear attack in an already-formed mêlée.

10. *Troops retreating from mêlée.* Such troops must throw a dice: 1, 2 or 3 they are routed and must form up one normal move directly back with their backs to the enemy, having been routed. If a 4, 5 or 6 is thrown then they are deemed to have retreated in an orderly fashion and form up facing the enemy.

11. *Standard bearers in mêlées.* If such a soldier is killed in a mêlée and his side lose the mêlée, thus having to retreat, it is considered that his standard is in danger of being captured. Player of retreating side throws dice—1, 2 or 3 dice throw means that standard is captured, whilst 4, 5 or 6 means that it is taken over by another bearer and saved.

MORALE

The introduction of morale factors in war games is an attempt to reproduce the intangible factor that causes a unit suddenly to break and retreat, to face up to and possibly beat a force much larger than itself, or to brace itself in spite of being attacked in flank or rear and having its officers killed. When certain predetermined situations occur the units concerned have to throw a dice to ascertain their subsequent behaviour. This inevitably means that luck plays the predominant part but, after all, war is a question of luck, uncertainty, chance and the like!

1. *Pre-contact morale.* If a unit is reduced to 50 per cent. by missile fire, if a unit on its immediate flank gives way and retreats, or if its officers are all killed, then that unit is considered possibly to have its morale affected and must throw a dice. If the dice falls 1 or 2, then the unit is considered to be shaken and must throw another dice to determine its subsequent course of action. Second dice throw: 5 or 6 means that it has rallied. 4 means that three-quarters of the unit run one move. 3 means that half of the unit run one move. 2 means that

all of the unit runs one move. 1 means that the whole unit runs two moves.

2. *Following a mêlée.* On conclusion of two rounds of mêlée fighting (one if overwhelming numbers or loss-of-officer rule prevails) both units involved throw a dice. If more than one unit on a side, then one dice per separate unit is thrown, so a force of three units, for example, would throw three morale dice.

If a 1 or 2 is thrown then the unit is considered shaken and a second dice must be thrown: 5 or 6 means unit is rallied. 3 or 4 means unit will retreat one move. 1 or 2 means that unit will retreat double move.

This is known as 'Contact Morale'.

3. *Subsequent action of units so affected.* When a unit is caused to retreat in this manner, in both pre-contact- and in contact-morale situations, an attempt to rally it must be made before it can take part in the next move.

If a 4, 5 or 6 is thrown then the unit is considered to have rallied, and it must remain stationary for that move but may turn and face enemy. If a 1, 2 or 3 is thrown, then the unit continues to run and will retreat another move appropriate to its arm.

A further attempt to rally it takes place before the next move, when it will take a 5 or 6 to rally it. If it fails again, then it will take another full move back. One last chance is given to rally the unit on the next move, when a 6 must be thrown, and if this is not obtained the unit must be permanently removed from the battlefield.

If, during the course of its retreat, a routed unit reaches the edge of the playing area then it must be removed from the battlefield.

4. *Staff officers* can be sent to aid in rallying a retreating unit, their presence adding one on to the dice score, so that on the first throw, for example, instead of a 4, 5 or 6 being required to rally the unit, a 3, 4, 5 or 6 will suffice. The presence of the commander-in-chief with a retreating unit will add *two* to its dice score. Having rallied a unit, however, the staff officer con-

cerned must remain with that unit for the remainder of the battle. Staff officers or C.-in-C. may move at the rate of 24 inches per move to reach a retreating unit.

5. *Overwhelming strength* (see Mêlées). Smaller unit throws one dice: 5 or 6 means it goes on fighting. 3 or 4 means it surrenders if no supporting unit within one infantry move of it, otherwise it retreats one move. 2 means whole unit bolts and is lost (dice thrown for each man who is saved by throw of 5 or 6). 1 means whole unit is cut down and lost.

6. *Flank attack* (see Mêlées). Unit attacked in flank throws one dice—5 or 6 means fights as normal. 4 means half fights, half runs (running half have to be diced for, 5 or 6 saves them). 3 means whole unit runs one move (has to be thrown for as above). 2 means whole unit surrenders and has to be escorted to enemy's rear with one enemy escort to every five captured. 1 means whole unit cut down and lost.

7. *Rear attacks* (see Mêlées). 6 means whole unit turns and fights. 4 or 5 means half unit fights, half runs (have to be thrown for). 2 or 3 means whole unit surrenders (see above). 1 means whole unit cut down and lost.

8. If the commander-in-chief of a force is killed or captured then every unit in that force must throw dice for their morale as in Pre-Contact Morale Section.

9. Infantry ranged 3 deep can add *one* on to their dice throw for morale purposes.

10. Guards units add *one* on to dice throw when attacked in flank or rear. Guards units cannot be routed at any time.

ELEPHANTS

1. *Elephants attacking infantry in three ranks.* Dice throw of 1 makes elephant swerve. If infantry in more than three ranks, dice throw of 1, 2 or 3 makes them swerve. Second dice throw decides direction of swerve—1 or 2 right, 3 or 4 left and 5 or 6 straight back. Elephant is then deemed to have stampeded.

2. *Stampeding elephant*. Any individuals in path of stamped-ing elephant are killed, any unit taken thus in flank or rear will lose a quarter of its strength and must throw for its morale. If a stampeding elephant runs frontally into an organized body of heavy infantry or cavalry, dice throw to see where it goes. 1 or 2 swerves right and continues in that direction moving further each game move, 3 or 4 swerves left and similarly continues, 5 or 6 plunges straight through unit, destroying one file, and unit must throw for morale.

3. *Elephant attacking home on heavy infantry*. Provided the elephant does not swerve, he will charge home on the ranks of infantry who must throw a dice to see if they withstand the charge. Infantry in more than 3 ranks need 3, 4, 5 or 6 to fight, infantry in 3 ranks need 4, 5 or 6 to fight, infantry in less than 3 ranks need 5 or 6. If the infantry do not stand but break each man must have a dice thrown for him—4, 5 or 6 to escape, 1, 2 or 3 trampled upon and out of battle. If infantry stand, throw one dice for every five men; if a 5 or 6 is thrown on any one dice throw again and second 5 or 6 in succession ham-strings elephant, putting it out of battle. One dice is thrown for each elephant and total scored represents men killed, thus a 5 on dice means five men killed.

4. *Elephants against light infantry or heavy infantry in less than three ranks*. Infantry need 5 or 6 to stand and fight, mêlée then carried out as above.

5. *Elephants against cavalry*. If cavalry belong to army that does not habitually contain elephants, so that the horses are unused to them, then the cavalry must throw 4, 5, or 6 to stand. If horses are used to elephants then they do not need to throw dice but stand automatically. If cavalry stand, 4 of them fight each elephant with straight dice throw, highest score wins. If cavalry beaten they are killed, if elephant beaten throw another dice—4, 5 or 6 elephant unhurt, 2 or 3 soldiers on elephant killed, 1 elephant killed. If cavalry break, dice throw for every man—4, 5 or 6 saves; 1, 2 or 3 killed.

6. *Elephant against elephant*. Straight dice throw, highest score wins and loser is killed.

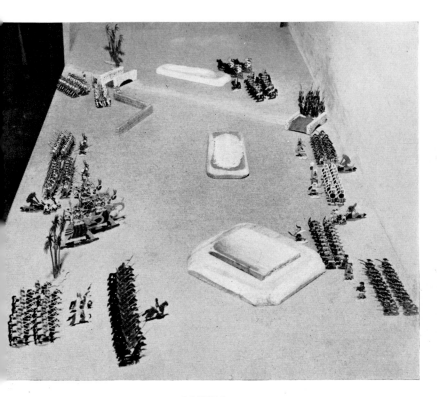

PLATE I

'THE ANCIENT BATTLE OF TRIMSOS'

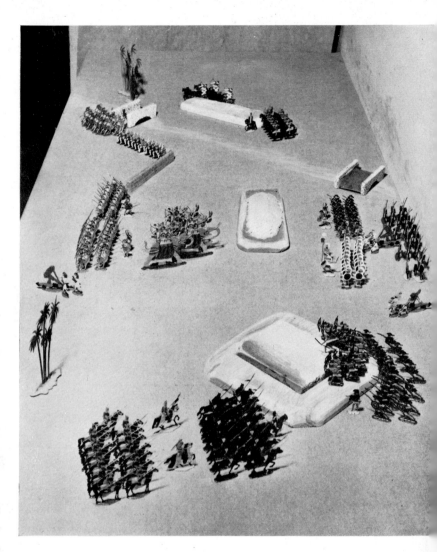

PLATE 2

PLATE 3

PLATE 4

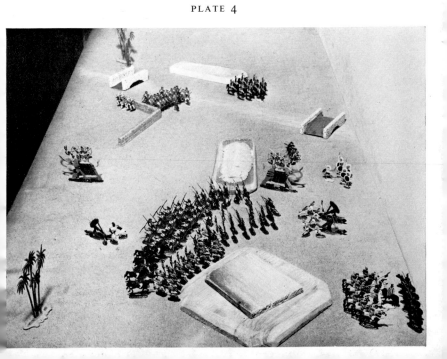

PLATE 5

7. *Light troops remaining within 12 inches of elephant.* Without 3 ranks of heavy troops between them must throw for morale at end of game move and before they can fire. They are shaken by 1, 2 or 3 and must again throw as per Pre-Contact Morale scale.

8. *Elephants hit by missiles.* Elephants can be hit by siege engines at normal range, but no further than 12-inch range by hand missiles.

Hits by siege engines, throw dice: 1 or 2 elephant and riders killed. 3 or 4 elephant wounded, remains stationary, riders unhurt. 5 or 6 elephant unhurt.

Hits by hand missiles, throw dice: 1 stampedes. 2 killed but men unhurt. 3 wounded, remains stationary. 4, 5 or 6 unhurt.

CHARIOTS

1. *Chariots against infantry.* If infantry are in double ranks or more, chariots throw dice and need 4, 5 or 6 to charge home, one dice being tossed for each chariot. If chariot does not charge home, throw further dice: 1, 2 or 3 chariot swerves to right and completes its move distance, 4, 5 or 6 chariot will swerve to left and continue its full move distance. If the chariot charges home, the infantry will throw dice and need 3, 4, 5 or 6 to stand. If they run, all in the path of the chariot will need dice thrown and only those who throw a 6 will escape. If infantry stand, chariot fights number of men equal to number of horses and men in chariot, one dice throw per group. If chariot is beaten, throw dice for horses and occupants of chariot individually—5 or 6 to save—if horse is killed the chariot is useless but men may dismount and fight on foot.

2. *Chariots against cavalry.* Throw a dice for each side, if cavalry throw a 1 they turn and bolt and need to throw a 5 or 6 individually to survive. If chariot throws a 1, then throw dice individually for each chariot—1 overturns, 2 bolts full move, 3 or 4 swerves full move right, 5 or 6 swerves full move left. If they engage, each chariot fights two cavalry.

3. *Chariots against chariots.* Both sides toss dice, if one throws 1 then that side swerves and no combat. Otherwise, throw dice first for each chariot on both sides, any throwing 5 or 6 collides and overturns, after that it is chariot against chariot, straight dice throw, highest score wins.

4. *Casualties from missile fire.* Number chariots and then throw dice to see which chariot is hit and how many times. Then throw again to see whether it is the driver, soldiers or a horse that is affected.* If driver or soldiers, they can be saved by 5 or 6. If horse or driver is killed, chariot overturns and kills all occupants.

5. *Chariot against elephant.* Elephants cannot be attacked by chariots but an elephant can trample two chariots in one move provided they are within his move range.

ANCIENT WARFARE: 'THE BATTLE OF TRIMSOS'

HYPERBOREA AGAINST HYRKANIA

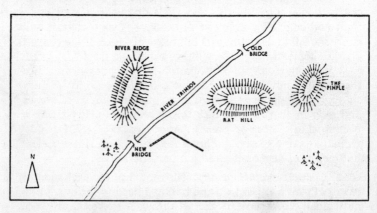

* Dice throws of 1 and 2 indicate horses hit. 3 indicates driver hit. 4 indicates archer hit. 5 and 6 is chariot itself.

This battle was fought in an undefined period of the chequered history of the mythical continent of Hyboria—a vast land mass dreamed up by Tony Bath of Southampton, which contains nations of almost every type of known warrior of our own world in its earliest times. These countries fight each other on the slightest provocation, make pacts, break pacts, invade, repel and generally carry on much as did our own ancestors in the earliest recorded days of history.

In this particular instance, Hyperborea and Hyrkania had a trivial frontier disagreement, leading to the despatch of two small punitive expeditions, who finally met in the arid region around the River Trimsos—how they fared will be seen as the battle unfolds.

The figures used are flat figures from Tony Bath's large collection. Perfectionists might detect some slight deviation in their respective periods or eras, but what are a few hundred years amongst so many? The terrain was erected on a board 6 feet by 3 feet, the narrowness causing all move distances to be halved to make for a better battle. It has always seemed to the author that Flats, particularly ancient Flats, possess a certain air of symbolism which makes them very distant cousins to chessmen—but chessmen of the best sort, carved in rare materials to accurate likenesses of knights, kings and the like. Therefore, when laying out the terrain for this battle, little attempt was made to make it realistic as was done with the other two battles described in this book. Hills were given a regular, stepped appearance, the river (which could be crossed only at the bridges) was denoted by a narrow, blue-chalked path and the trees, playing little useful part, merely denoted that the area over which so much 'blood' was to be spilt was somewhere in the tropics.

The respective armies were formed as follows:

Hyperborea:

1 regiment each of the following infantry (each 20 men):

The Thurn Archers

2nd Gwalur Infantry

1st Gwalur Infantry

1st Thurn Infantry.

1 regiment each of the following cavalry (15 men each):

1st Guard Cavalry

2nd Hyperborea Mounted Archers

3 War Chariots

1 Heavy War Engine

1 Light War Engine.

Hyrkania:

1 regiment each of the following infantry (20 men each):

2nd Imperial Archers

1st Imperial Foot Guards

2nd Imperial Foot Guards

3rd Imperial Foot Guards.

1 regiment each of the following cavalry (15 men each):

1st Fort Ghori Cavalry

2nd Imperial Light Horse

3 War Elephants

1 Heavy War Engine.

Initial dispositions of both armies can be seen in *Plate 1*. On the left of the photograph is massed the Hyrkanian Army, with their opponents, the Hyperboreans, on the right.

In the immediate foreground can be seen the Hyrkanian leading unit, the 2nd Imperial Light Horse, formed in single line and screening their heavier comrades, the 1st Fort Ghori Cavalry. Beyond them are the dreaded War Elephants, trumpeting madly as they thunder forward. Behind them the sweating crew laboriously draw forward their War Engine, with on their left flank the 1st Imperial Foot Guards, then the 3rd Imperial Foot Guards. The 2nd Imperial Archers can be seen moving into position behind the stone wall whilst their heavy infantry, the 2nd Imperial Foot Guards, take up their stand by the New Bridge.

To counter this threatening formation, the Hyperboreans have assumed the following dispositions: On the far side of the River Trimsos, beyond River Ridge, their War Chariots begin an outflanking movement, backed up by the 2nd Hyperborean Mounted Archers. Realizing that such a separation of forces is a risky business, the Hyperborean commander has urgently recalled the 1st Guard Cavalry who were originally also part of the outflanking force, and they are making their way back to the main body over the Old Bridge. The Hyperborean main force, reading from the foreground, consists of the 2nd Gwalur Infantry, on their right, and in advance of them the Thurn Archers move forward to get into position on the Pimple. A light War Engine is being dragged forward in the gap between the Archers and the 1st Thurn Infantry, whilst the heavier War Engine slowly trundles forward to the left of the last unit, the 1st Gwalur Infantry.

It must be realized when looking at this plate that the apparent nearness of each army to the other at such an early stage in the battle is due to the narrowness of the table on which the game was being played. As has already been stated, to counter this all moves were halved in distance; nevertheless such a narrow battlefield has a definite advantage when one wishes the battle to quickly get under way and desires a result in a fairly short period of time. Any disadvantages in tactical movements caused by the scarcity of space is offset by the battle being hectic and exciting from the word 'Go'.

1st Game Move

Hyrkania won the toss and decided that Hyperborea should move first.

Hyperborean moves

Every unit moved a double move except the Mounted Archers. Thus: the War Chariots moved south in the shelter of the western side of River Ridge. The Mounted Archers sheltered at the northern end of River Ridge. The 1st Guard Cavalry hastily trotted off in a north-easterly direction, towards the Old Bridge, with the idea of reinforcing their main body. The Thurn Archers moved directly forward towards the northern end of the Pimple, with the 2nd Gwalur Infantry behind them and to their left. The 1st Gwalur and 1st Thurn Infantry moved directly forward in the direction of Rat Hill, with the War Engines behind them.

Hyrkanian moves
The 2nd Imperial Archers moved forward a double move (all units moved double) and took up a position near the southern end of the stone wall. Following them, and moving towards the New Bridge, came the 2nd Imperial Foot Guards. The 1st and 3rd Imperial Foot Guards went forward directly northwards in the direction of Rat Hill, with their War Engine on their right. Making for the gap between Rat Hill and the Pimple, the three War Elephants rumbled forward. On their right and to the eastward side of the Pimple went the cavalry, 1st Fort Ghori and 2nd Imperial Light Horse. *There was no firing on this move.*

2nd Game Move
Hyperborea won the toss and decided that Hyrkania should move first.

Hyrkanian moves
2nd Imperial Foot Guards take up position at entrance to New Bridge. 2nd Imperial Archers line north-west leg of stone wall facing across river. The 1st and 3rd Imperial Foot Guards continue marching forward towards Rat Hill with their War Engine on their right. The War Elephants have now reached the southern edge of Rat Hill at its right-hand corner. The 2nd Imperial Light Horse trot forward to the eastern side of the Pimple at about its middle, whilst the other cavalry unit, the 1st Fort Ghori Cavalry, are a little behind them.

Hyperborean moves
Chariots move forward still in shelter of western side of River

Ridge. The Mounted Archers move forward, east of River Ridge, to a point about half-way down the length of the Ridge —they do a split move and fire as below.

The 1st Guard Cavalry move directly eastwards behind their own infantry towards the Pimple. The 1st Gwalur and 1st Thurn Infantry move forward towards Rat Hill, with their War Engines in their rear. The Thurn Archers began to ascend the northern slopes of the Pimple, with the 2nd Gwalur Infantry behind them. *Plate 2* shows the situation at the end of the 2nd Game Move.

The 2nd Imperial Light Horse of the Hyrkanian Army have now formed into two ranks and are advancing rapidly round the eastern end of the Pimple, followed closely by the 1st Fort Ghori Cavalry. Hastily moving on to the top of the Pimple, the Thurn Archers make ready to oppose them, whilst being protected on the lower slopes by the 2nd Gwalur Infantry. It is evident that these infantry units are fervently hoping that their own cavalry, the 1st Guard Cavalry, having been recalled from the flank force, will arrive in time to handle the Hyrkanian horsemen. In this can be seen a typical example of the lack of team spirit that seemed to pervade this Hyperborean force throughout the battle.

The elephants are moving fast towards Rat Hill, the shallow slopes of which will in no way handicap the mighty animals in their crushing progress. The Thurn Infantry and the 1st Gwalur Infantry of the Hyperborean force evidently hoped to be on top of Rat Hill before the elephants hit them, but it is quite evident that they will not do so—they would, in fact, do very much better if they rapidly formed themselves into a four-deep square in an effort to fight off the elephants.

The remainder of the Hyrkanian Heavy Infantry are steadily moving forward in the rear of the elephants to be used to mop up the Hyperborean infantry after the elephants have hit them—in this they take a calculated risk because, should the elephants be turned back, they might well stampede directly through their own infantry!

On the Hyrkanian left flank the 2nd Imperial Foot Guards have now got into position to hold the New Bridge, and it appears as though the War Chariots intend directly rushing the bridge, a big obstacle because of its narrowness. The Mounted Archers have carried out a split move, moving forward from the position in which they can now be seen to a point within 12-inch range of the Imperial Archers sheltering behind the stone wall. The fire of the Mounted Archers was devastating and they immediately killed seven of the archers in spite of their stone-wall shelter. The Imperial Archers had the chance to take revenge on the Mounted Archers, but were apparently so shaken by their losses that they killed only one of them.

The trend of the battle is now becoming apparent and, unless the chariots succeed quickly in forcing the New Bridge, to permit the Mounted Archers to come through and occupy the Hyrkanian Heavy Infantry before too much damage is done by the elephants and the cavalry, the Hyperborean chances look slim.

Firing.

As Hyrkania were first-movers, Hyperborea fired first.

1. As already stated, the Mounted Archers did a split move and fired 3 volleys at 12-inch range, their target being the 2nd Imperial Archers (behind the stone wall). 8 hits were scored. The archers, being unarmoured men, have to throw a 6 to be saved, plus in this case, because of the stone-wall shelter, an extra 1. They managed to save only 1 man.

2. The 2nd Imperial Archers threw dice to see if they were able to fire on the Mounted Archers as they came in at them—they threw a 6 and were thus able to fire their 13 remaining men. They fired at 12-inch range—having 2 volleys and 3 odd men—and scored 6 hits on the Mounted Archers, whose saving throws were phenomenally lucky in that only 1 mounted archer was killed. *At this stage no one else was in a position to fire.*

3rd Game Move

Hyperborea won dice throw for move—decided to move first because of nearness of Hyrkanian elephants and cavalry.

Hyperborean moves

Chariots charged over the New Bridge and made mêlée contact with the 2nd Imperial Foot Guards holding the eastern end of the bridge. Mounted Archers moved down eastern side of River Ridge, getting into position to fire upon the stone wall and its sheltering archers. The 1st Thurn and 1st Gwalur Infantry moved forward to the foot of the rear slopes of Rat Hill. The War Engines took up firing positions in much the same place as they had attained during the last move. The 1st Guard Cavalry arrived at the rear of the Pimple, where they formed into line of battle. The Thurn Archers took up firing positions on the crest of the Pimple with the 2nd Gwalur Infantry split into two protective forces on both flanks, a little lower down the hill so that they could be fired over.

Hyrkanian moves

The 2nd Imperial Foot Guards remained in position at entrance to New Bridge, resisting the attack of the chariots upon them. The 2nd Imperial Archers (now 13 in number) continued to line the brick wall. The 1st and 3rd Imperial Foot Guards now reached the rear slopes (southern side) of Rat Hill but had not commenced the ascent. The War Engine remained in firing position some distance back. The 2nd Imperial Light Horse, being fired upon by the Thurn Archers, moved round the Pimple and attacked the 1st Guard Cavalry, being supported in this attack by the 1st Fort Ghori Cavalry. The three War Elephants thundered up the gentle slopes of Rat Hill, over the crest and down the other side to charge into the two Hyperborean infantry units on the far side.

Plate 3 shows the situation at the end of the 3rd game move (before firing and mêlées took place).

The Hyrkanian Cavalry, who probably did not intend to attack the strong infantry concentration on the Pimple anyway, moved away from them and attacked the 1st Guard Cavalry, who had arrived and taken up a position in rear of the Pimple —giving the highly favourable situation of two units against one, the two units also having impetus bonus! The Hyrkanians

F

will, of course, have to take fire from the Thurn Archers on the Pimple as they pass the hill.

As anticipated, the elephants got to Rat Hill and thundered over its shallow slopes before the Hyperborean heavy infantry could begin to ascend. So that the elephants, in addition to their natural weight and velocity, have the advantage of thundering down the rear slopes into the infantry—two elephants charging into the 1st Thurn Infantry whilst one charged the 1st Gwalur Infantry. Both the Hyperborean War Engines will have the opportunity of firing on the elephants, provided the dice say that they are loaded! (It actually transpired that the light War Engine had not loaded, whilst the heavy War Engine had a great success when it scored a direct hit on the elephant attacking the 1st Gwalur Infantry, killing it immediately.)

The chariots did charge over the New Bridge, to be met by the 2nd Imperial Foot Guards formed up in readiness. The Imperial Archers, from behind their stone wall, fired a deadly volley on the chariots as they came in and destroyed two of them (although these chariots had previously thrown dice to see if they charged home on the infantry and had, in fact, earned the right to do so). But Chariot No. 1 had met with disaster in a different way—escaping the arrows of the archers it had refused to charge home on the infantry and, squeezing past them on their left flank, had gone careering on down river (it can be seen in the top left-hand corner of the plate).

The Mounted Archers caused more casualties on the Imperial Archers behind the wall, killing 4 of them and reducing them to 9 in number. Although such reduction in the Hyrkanian Light Infantry was valuable, it in no way reflected the true threat that such a strong force of Mounted Archers should have been to the Hyrkanians.

Firing
Hyperborea was first-mover therefore Hyrkania fires first.

1. 2nd Imperial Archers wish to fire on chariots attacking 2nd Imperial Foot Guards—throw dice to ascertain range— throw 5 so fire at 6-inch range. 2 volleys and 3 odd men score

4 hits on chariots. Dice thrown to see effect of hits, which works out at 3 hits on Chariot No. 2 and 1 hit on Chariot No. 3.

Chariot 2. 1 hit on horse, 1 hit on driver and 1 hit on chariot itself—saving throws denote both driver and horse are killed—therefore Chariot No. 2 is destroyed and out of action.

Chariot 3. Hit on horse, which is killed, therefore this chariot is also out of action.

(The chariots threw dice to see if they charged home on the 2nd Imperial Foot Guards who were massed two-deep. Chariot 1 refused and swerved right after it had crossed the bridge. Chariots 2 and 3 charged home—but, as both were destroyed, the attack has failed.)

2. Hyrkanian War Engine wishes to fire on Thurn Archers, who are situated on the Pimple—as it has not yet fired it is considered to be loaded so dice thrown for effect—3, so it is a *miss*.

3. *Hyperborean firing.* Mounted Archers fire on 2nd Imperial Archers at 12-inch range—2 volleys and 4 odd men—score 5 hits. Archers' saving throw—they lose 4.

4. Heavy War Engine firing on elephants at 6-inch range—scores 4 so has *hit* Elephant No. 1—dice thrown for effect—2, so elephant and riders destroyed.

5. Light War Engine firing on Elephant No. 2—throws 2, so misses.

6. Thurn Archers firing on Hyrkanian Cavalry as they move past Pimple to attack Hyperborean Cavalry. 4 volleys—2 on each unit of cavalry at 6-inch range—7 hits on 2nd Imperial Light Horse of which 2 are saved so 5 are killed. 4 hits on Fort Ghori Cavalry of which 1 is killed.

Mêlées

1. No. 2 Elephant throws dice to see if it charges home on 1st Thurn Infantry (in three ranks)—throws 6, so does charge home. No. 3 Elephant throws 4, so also charges home—both elephants charging 1st Thurn Infantry.

Infantry now throw to see if they stand against the charge of the elephants (need 4, 5, 6 for each elephant). They throw 4 and 4—so they stand. Infantry throw 1 dice for every 5 men so throw 4 dice—3, 2, 3, 5. Under Rule 3, in Section 'Elephants', throw 5 scoring dice again but throw 1 this time so no damage done to elephants.

Elephants throw 1 dice per elephant—throw 1 and 4 so have killed 5 infantry (for whom there is no saving throw in this case). Both elephants are deemed to have broken through infantry ranks and are moved to the rear of the unit. Thurn Infantry now throw dice for their morale standing—throw 2, which means they are 'shaken'—throw second dice—3, which indicates that they must retreat 1 move—final dice throw of 6 denotes that it was an orderly retreat and they face the enemy.

1st Gwalur Infantry on their right flank must also throw dice for their morale standing, as their flank unit has broken (see Pre-Contact Morale, rule 1). Throw 4, therefore they are sound and stand fast.

2. *Hyrkanian Cavalry attack Hyperborean 1st Guard Cavalry.*

1st Round

Hyrkanian Cavalry

2nd Imp. Light Horse (10 men) ⎱ Total of 24 men = 5 dice
1st Fort Ghori Cavalry (14 men) ⎰ (+impetus bonus).

Hyperborean Cavalry

1st Guard Cavalry (15 men)   15 men or 3 dice.

Hyrkania dice scores—3, 3, 2, 2, 5 + 1 per dice for impetus = 20 or 10 men hit.

Hyperborea dice scores—5, 2, 1 = 8, or 4 men hit.

Saving throws. Hyrkania saved 2, lost 2 cavalry.
                        Hyperborea saved 7, lost 3 cavalry.

2nd Round

Hyrkania

8 Light Cavalry ⎱ Total 22 men = 4½ dice to throw. 4, 6, 2,
14 Heavy Cavalry ⎰ 3 + half of 2 = 16, or 8 hits.

Hyperborea

12 Heavy Cavalry—Totals $2\frac{1}{2}$ dice$=6$, 1 and half of $2=8$, or 4 cavalry hit.

Saving throws. Hyrkania lose 2 Light Horse killed. 1 officer and 2 Heavy Cavalry killed.

Hyperborea lose 3 cavalry.

Thus, at end of mêlée, state of combatants is as follows:

Hyrkania have 6 remaining of 2nd Imperial Light Horse and 11 of the 1st Fort Ghori Cavalry (less an officer).

Hyperborea have 9 remaining of 1st Guard Cavalry.

Morale. Hyrkanian Light Cavalry throw 2, then 3, so they retreat one full move. 1st Fort Ghori Cavalry throw 4, so stand ground.

Hyperborean Cavalry throw 2, then 4, so they retreat one full move.

4th Game Move

Hyrkania won move dice throw and decided to move first. Before moving, threw morale dice to see course of action of 2nd Imperial Light Horse (forced to retreat last move). Dice score 4—which rallies cavalry but they may not move this game move.

2nd Imperial Foot Guards at New Bridge (having repelled attack by chariots) form into ranks so that half are facing over bridge and other half facing chariot that swerved past them.

2nd Imperial Archers (now down to 9 men) remain on stone wall.

Elephant No. 2 attacks 1st Gwalur Infantry at rear of Rat Hill whilst Elephant No. 3 moves forward and again attacks 1st Thurn Infantry who were beaten back last move.

The 1st and 3rd Imperial Foot Guards move into position at the eastern end of Rat Hill.

The 1st Fort Ghori Cavalry again charge into the 1st Guard Cavalry, whom they assisted in beating last move, whilst the 2nd Imperial Light Horse remain in the position well east of the Pimple to which they retreated after the last move.

The War Engine moves forward and is ready for firing.

Hyperborean moves

The chariot that swerved during its last move attack turns and charges again into the re-formed 2nd Imperial Foot Guards. The Mounted Archers move south-west, cross New Bridge, mêlée with infantry.

The 1st Guard Cavalry remain in the position to which they retreated during the last move and are attacked again by 1st Fort Ghori Cavalry.

The Thurn Archers and 2nd Gwalur Infantry remain in their positions on the Pimple, whilst the 1st Gwalur and 1st Thurn Infantry are again attacked by elephants before they can move.

War Engines remain in same position.

Firing

Having moved last, Hyperborea fire first.

1. Chariot containing 1 archer fires at 6-inch range on 2nd Imperial Foot Guards whom it is attacking—scores 1 hit, but saving throw of 5 means no men killed.

2. Mounted Archers fire 1 volley at 2nd Imperial Archers at 6-inch range—score 1 hit—saving throw denotes 1 man killed. 9 Mounted Archers fire at 2nd Imperial Foot Guards before they mêlée with them—1 volley and 4 odd men = at 6-inch range, 7 men hit. Infantry saving throw—lost 4.

3. Thurn Archers (on Pimple) 2 volleys at 12-inch range on 2nd Imperial Light Horse—3 hits—saving throw 1 killed. 2 volleys also on 1st Imperial Foot Guards at 6-inch range—scored 8 hits—saving throws—1 officer and 1 man killed.

4. War Engine throws 4 so is loaded. Fires at Elephant No. 3—at 6-inch range throws 3 = *miss*.

5. Light War Engine throws 3—therefore considered unloaded.

Hyrkanian firing

1. 2 Imperial Archers (4 men) fire on chariot at 12-inch range—score 1 hit—(dice thrown to see what is hit—4 means

that it is an archer within chariot—saving throw 1 archer killed).

2. War Engine—throws 6, so is loaded—fires on archers on Pimple at 12-inch range—dice score 5 means *hit*—all troops within 4-in. radius of where missile dropped (i.e. 7 men) are hit. Saving throws: 1 officer and 4 men killed of Thurn Archers.

3. Archers on elephants (3 on each). Elephant No. 2 firing on 1st Gwalur Infantry at 6 inches scores 2 hits. Saving throw 1 killed. Elephant No. 3 firing at 6 inches on 1st Thurn Infantry—scores 1 hit. Saving throw: 1 man killed.

Mêlées

1. Chariot into 2nd Imperial Foot Guards on New Bridge (who are in four ranks, two facing each way). Chariot throws 2, so again refuses to charge home. Then throws 5, so it swerves left—into river—where it is destroyed.

2. Mounted Archers attacking 2nd Imperial Foot Guards on Bridge—Mounted Archers throw dice to see if they charge home—throw 2 so they refuse to charge, throw 3, which means they swerve right towards Palm Trees.

3. Elephant No. 2 has to throw to see if it charges home on 1st Gwalur Infantry as they are formed up in three ranks. Throws 1, so elephant swerves—second throw of 5 sends elephant straight back, so that it will eventually run off field.

4. Elephant No. 3—throws 2, so attacks 1st Thurn Infantry, who throw to see if they stand fast—throw 2 which means that they break. (In this case a saving throw must be made for each man of the unit—14 remain—5 escape and 9 are trampled to death, 5 survivors retreat in routed condition.)

5. 1st Fort Ghori Cavalry against 1st Guard Cavalry:

1st Round. Hyrkanian Cavalry have 11 men = 2 dice (+ bonus for impetus)—score 3 hits.

Hyperborean Cavalry have 8 men—throw 1½ dice, score 3 hits.

Saving throws. Hyrkania 1 man killed.
　　　　　　Hyperborea all saved.

2nd Round. Hyrkania have 10 men = 2 dice = 5 hits.
　　　　　　Hyperborea have 8 men = 1½ dice = 2 hits.

Saving throws. Hyrkania lose 1 man.
　　　　　　Hyperborea lose 3 men.

　　Thus at end of mêlée, Hyrkania have 9 men left, whilst Hyperborea have 5 men left.

Morale. Hyrkania score 2, 5—so stand fast.
　　　　　Hyperborea score 4—so stand fast.

5th Game Move

　　Hyperborea win move dice throw—move first.

　　1. Mounted Archers move north-east towards Old Bridge

　　2. 1st Gwalur Infantry move north-east and make contact with 1st Imperial Foot Guards immediately east of Rat Hill.

　　3. War Engines remain in position.

　　4. 1st ·Thurn Infantry (5 survivors) throw for morale but still fall back towards baseline.

　　5. 1st Guard Cavalry (5 men) are still engaged with 1st Fort Ghori Cavalry (9 men).

　　6. 2nd Gwalur Infantry come off Pimple and attack 3rd Imperial Foot Guards.

　　7. Thurn Archers (16 men) come off Pimple and attack 1st Imperial Foot Guards (after firing on them first—see later).

Hyrkanian moves

　　1. 2nd Imperial Foot Guard move north-east to front of stone wall in direction of main battle .Surviving Imperial Archers (4 only) remain in position behind stone wall.

　　Plate 4 illustrates the situation at the 5th Game Move—before firing and mêlées took place, and it can be seen that things look very black for the Hyperborean Army!

　　The 1st Guard Cavalry, having been beaten back in their

original mêlée with both the Heavy and Light Hyrkanian Cavalry, have again been engaged by the 1st Fort Ghori Cavalry and the mêlée continues near the Hyperborean baseline. This is the second move over which the mêlée has stretched. The 2nd Imperial Light Horse, not being needed in the above mêlée, have moved back and are taking part in the big and, could be, final mêlée between Rat Hill and the Pimple.

Here it can be seen that the Thurn Archers and the 2nd Gwalur Infantry have come down from their strong positions on the Pimple and have attacked the 1st and 3rd Imperial Foot Guards, who had moved directly east of Rat Hill so that, if unopposed, they would have had the Hyperborean War Engines at their mercy.

The situation is a little confused in the centre, the elephant has moved towards the few survivors of the 1st Thurn Infantry, but in a few minutes he will be hit by a missile from one of the War Engines and so badly wounded that he will not move from the spot. The second remaining elephant is still hot-footing it back towards his own baseline and will continue to run until he leaves the field of battle—elephants are formidable opponents but sometimes can be a little unpredictable.

Behind the attacking elephant can be seen the three survivors of the 1st Gwalur Infantry who attacked the 1st Imperial Foot Guard and were repulsed with very heavy losses—in their panic they retreated back to their original position instead of moving directly backwards to aid in covering their War Engines. Behind them are the 5 survivors of the 1st Thurn Infantry who have suffered grievously in their contact with the elephants.

Over on the far side of the battlefield, the Hyrkanians have triumphed completely, the chariots have been destroyed, and the Mounted Archers are making a futile attempt to rejoin their main body in time to give some assistance. Relieved of the need to guard the New Bridge, the 2nd Imperial Foot Guard are moving rapidly forward to reinforce the rest of their army—but it does not look as though they will be required even if it were possible for them to arrive in time. The few gallant survivors of the Imperial Archers rest exhausted behind their stone wall.

Elephant No. 2 continues his stampede back towards his own baseline. Elephant No. 3 charges towards War Engines. 1st and 3rd Imperial Foot Guards are engaged in mêlée immediately east of Rat Hill with the Thurn Archers and the 2nd Gwalur Infantry. The 2nd Imperial Light Horse move round the Pimple to take part in this mêlée, engaging part of the Thurn Archers.

The 1st Fort Ghori Horse are still engaged in a mêlée with the 1st Foot Guards north of the Pimple near the Hyperborean baseline.

Firing

Hyrkania fires first—War Engine throws 2 = *not loaded*.

2. Archers on Elephant No. 3—3 men at 6-inch range firing on War Engine crews—score 1 hit—saving throw—no casualties.

3. Hyperborea firing—archers on Pimple fire on Hyrkanian Infantry before mêléeing with them—throw for distance and score for 6-inch range—3 volleys and 1 odd man—score 14 hits. Saving throws—1st Imperial Foot Guards lose 2 officers and 5 men.

4. War Engines on Elephant No. 3 at 6-inch range. Dice throws indicate that one engine is loaded—throws for hit—scores 6 which is hit on No. 3 Elephant—means that he cannot move although his riders are unhurt.

Mêlées

1. 1st Fort Ghori Cavalry (9 men) against 1st Guard Cavalry (5 men).

1st Round. Fort Ghori Cavalry: 2 dice—score 2 hits.
       Guard Cavalry: 1 dice—score 3 hits.

Saving throws. Fort Ghori Cavalry lose 1.
       Guard Cavalry lose none.

2nd Round. Fort Ghori Cavalry (8 men)—1½ dice—score 3 hits.
       Guard Cavalry (5 men)—1 dice—score 3 hits.

Saving throws. Fort Ghori Cavalry lose 2 men.
                Guard Cavalry lose 2 men.

Therefore, at end of mêlée, Fort Ghori Cavalry have 6 men left and Guard Cavalry have 3 men left—Fort Ghori Cavalry claim 'Overwhelming Numbers'—Guard Cavalry throw 3, which means surrender if no supporting troops within an infantry move—there are none so Guard Cavalry survivors surrender. Fort Ghori Cavalry detail 2 men to guard prisoners and have 4 men remaining for next move.

2. Thurn Infantry attack 1st Imperial Foot Guard. Thurn Infantry have 19 men—4 dice (plus impetus bonus)—score 8 hits.

Imperial Foot Guard have 20 men—4 dice—score 6 hits.

Saving throws. Thurn Infantry lose 1 officer and 5 men.
                Imperial Foot Guard lose 2 men.

2nd Round. Thurn Infantry (13 men) have 2½ dice—score 3 hits.
            Imperial Foot Guards (18 men) 3½ dice—score 8 hits.

Saving throws. Thurn Infantry lose 1 officer and 3 men.
                Imperial Foot Guards lose no men.

Therefore, at end of 2nd round of fighting, Thurn Infantry have 9 survivors whilst Imperial Foot Guards have 18 men left. The Imperial Foot Guards thus claim 'Overwhelming Numbers'.

Thurn Infantry throw dice—2, which means that the whole unit bolts—each man having to be individually diced for (5 or 6 saves). Result of this saving throw—3 men left. The survivors retreat.

3. Thurn Archers (16 men) and 2nd Gwalur Infantry (10 men) against 3rd Imperial Foot Guards (18 men) plus Imperial Light Horse (5 men).

As the Hyperboreans attacked they have impetus bonus, but as Imperial Light Horse also attacked before mêlée had begun they too get similar bonus.

Hyrkania have 18 points for their infantry, plus 10 points for their cavalry, which gives them 28 points or 5½ dice—

impetus bonus of 1 per dice being added to 2 dice for cavalry. Score 18, which gives 9 hits.

Hyperborea have 26 infantry all with impetus bonus—5 dice—score 18 which means 9 points hit.

Saving throws. Hyrkania lose 1 cavalryman and 2 infantry.
Hyperborea lose 4 archers and 2 Heavy Infantry.

2nd Round

Hyrkania now have 4 cavalry and 16 infantry—24 points—5 dice—score 18 or 9 hits.

Hyperborea now have 20 infantry (no impetus bonus second round)—4 dice—score 20 or 10 points hit.

Saving throws. *Hyrkania* lose 1 officer and 1 man infantry.
Hyperborea lose 1 officer and 5 archers, 3 Heavy Infantry.

Morale: Hyrkania. Imperial Light Horse 4—Stand Fast.
3rd Imperial Foot Guards 5—Stand Fast.

Hyperborea. Thurn Archers 1, shaken: 2nd dice 2 means this unit retreats a double move.
2nd Gwalur Infantry—2, which means that they are 'shaken': 2nd dice is 3, which indicates that this unit will retreat one infantry move.

(The double-move retreat of the Thurn Archers, being carried out directly backwards, resulted in them retreating completely off the table over their own baseline—thus they are lost to the battle.)

End of 5th Game Move

Before the 6th game could take place the Hyperborean commander, realizing that he had no chance of saving the battle, conceded the contest and his force retreated from the field.

Plate 5. Showing the final position of troops of both sides after the firing and mêlées of the 5th Game Move had ended. It was at this stage that the Hyperborean commander decided discretion to be the better part of valour and conceded the battle.

In the immediate right foreground the remaining 1st Fort Ghori Cavalry have just vanquished the 1st Guard Cavalry. The 2nd Gwalur Infantry have been backed against the Pimple, after coming off worst in the mêlée against Hyrkanian Imperial Foot Guards aided by Light Cavalry, their archers having been sent routed from the field.

The 1st and 3rd Imperial Foot Guards with the remnants of the Imperial Light Horse hold their position and are poised to advance.

The elephants are seen, one rushing madly from the field in a mad stampede whilst the other stands wounded and motionless in the position in which he was hit.

The Hyperborean infantry, the 1st Thurn and the 1st Gwalur, pitifully few in number, have been forced back almost on to their own baseline. Their friendly cavalry, the Mounted Archers, might possibly affect the situation if they came over the Bridge and made contact with the enemy, but the decision was taken out of their hands by their commander's withdrawal decision.

The 2nd Imperial Foot Guards, in full strength, are moving across the table towards the battle, after their most successful defence of the New Bridge.

Both side's War Engines remain in their firing positions.

7

Horse-and-Musket Warfare

RULES AND DEMONSTRATION BATTLE: 'ACTION IN THE PLATTVILLE VALLEY'

PLAYERS dice first to determine which army takes first move —the army moving second always fires first.

The Move

Line Infantry	6 inches	May move double distance when-
Light Infantry	9 inches	ever desired but may *not* fire that
Guard Infantry	6 inches	move. This double move can never
Cavalry	18 inches	be taken when hills are to be
Artillery	12 inches	climbed or river crossings made.
Horse Artillery	18 inches	
Transport	6 inches	
Staff Officers	24 inches	

1. All arms receive 3-inch distance bonus when moving on roads.

2. Only Light Infantry can move through woods, uphill, through marshland, etc., at their normal move rate. All other arms move at single rate on these occasions. Troops do *not* receive double moves when proceeding through woods, uphill over marshland, etc.

3. Artillery may move half their normal distance and still fire. A gun takes 3 inches to limber or unlimber.

4. All fences, walls, etc., that are deemed climbable take 3

inches off their move to climb by infantry, both light and line, and by cavalry.

5. When a unit is moving forward it must have its officers and standard bearer in front. They may only be in rear of unit when it has not moved on that particular move.

6. *Rivers:* Rivers are classified as under; this classification is made known before the battle commences:

Class A rivers. Take 6 inches to cross; during the crossing troops are not able to fire.

Class B rivers. Take 3 inches to cross; during this crossing troops may fire.

Guns and wagons can only cross Class A rivers by recognized bridges or ford.

Bridges can be crossed by two units per game move—one unit takes a double move and thus goes first, whilst second unit crosses on a single move and finishes up in rear of first unit.

7. Light Infantry may 'split move'—that is to say, they can move say 4 inches of their 9-inch move, fire and then move back 5 inches roughly to their original position, if desired.

8. Where cavalry are of the type that may fire their carbines or pistols they must take 3 inches of their move to dismount, 3 inches to fire and a further 3 inches to remount—thus leaving themselves with 9 inches of their move distance remaining. This does not apply if the cavalry fire from the saddle, when separate rules apply.

Firing

1. *Artillery:* A gun is crewed by four men who work under the following rules:

Gun may fire each move when crewed by 3 or 4 men.

Gun may fire alternate moves when crewed by 2 men.

Gun may fire every third move when crewed by 1 man.

A gun that has lost crew may be re-crewed by infantry who move to it in their normal move; such a procedure takes one move to carry out and the new crew cannot fire gun on that move.

Ammunition. Each gun has ten rounds per battle (coloured plastic counters being used). It may fire one round per move, subject to rules concerning hits and misses. If the gun misses with its first shot it may have one more shot that move if desired. When a shot is fired, a counter is given up to one's opponent. When a gun runs out of ammunition it can no longer fire unless ammunition from another gun is brought across under normal move conditions.

Firing artillery. When a gun is fired, the target is nominated and a dice is thrown. If the target is over 4 feet away from the gun then a hit is registered by throwing a 6 on the dice.

Target 3 to 4 feet   hit registered by 5 or 6

Target 2 to 3 feet   „   4, 5 or 6

Target 1 to 2 feet   „   3, 4, 5 or 6

Target 6 inches to 1 foot   „   2, 3, 4, 5 or 6

Target under 6 inches—hit is considered automatic.

When a hit is registered, the player throws *two* dice and the combined total is the number of casualties the shell has caused.

Gun firing on another gun. Throw as above to see if a hit is registered. If successful, throw two dice together:

Total 12: Gun and crew destroyed for remainder of battle.

Total 11: Ditto, *if* the gun is out in the open or in an exposed position. If the gun is under cover then 3 of crew are hit.

Total 10: Gun under cover has 2 of crew killed. Gun in open has 3 of crew killed.

Total 9: Gun under cover has 1 of crew killed. Gun in open has 2 of crew killed.

Total 8: Gun in open has 1 of crew killed.

Artillery crews cannot count gun as giving them cover.

Destruction of buildings, etc. Artillery can destroy houses, walls, bridges, etc., by throwing a dice total of *five*, the number of dice used to attain this score being as under:

At range of over 12 inches—1 dice.

At range of under 12 inches—2 dice.

At range of under 6 inches—3 dice.

Position of artillery when firing. Guns may fire over the heads of their own infantry provided the gun is at least 9 inches behind those troops. Otherwise can fire over own infantry if gun is sited on higher level such as hill-top. Guns have a range-angle latitude of 22½ degrees, thus a gun does not have to be *directly* pointed at its nominated target but is considered to have swivelled its muzzle.

Guns in mêlées. If a gun and its crew become involved in a mêlée, the crew fight as normal troops and the gun cannot fire that move. If the gun is overrun, then a dice is thrown and 4, 5 or 6 means retreating troops have managed to get their gun away; 2 or 3 means that the gun has been captured; 1 means that the crew have spiked the gun which is out of action for rest of game.

Artillery has unlimited range on the war-games table, being only restricted in its targets by natural obstacles such as hills being in the way, or by houses, etc.

Guns cannot fire on enemy over the heads of their own infantry if that enemy force is closer to friendly infantry than 9 inches. Unless a gun is on high ground, its target must be that enemy force its shell would first encounter. Thus, if the gun fires at a line of infantry, with a force of cavalry behind them, the shell *must* hit the infantry and the cavalry cannot be fired upon.

Mitrailleuse. Throw dice—1, 2, 3 entitles one dice for hits. 4, 5, 6 entitles two dice for hits. These dice are then thrown as infantry volleys at ranges following.

Infantry firing

A group of troops fires volleys in proportion to its numbers thus: Guards fire one volley for every four men. Light and Line troops fire volley for five men. Dismounted cavalry fire a volley for every five men but only three men out of every four can fire as the fourth man is considered to be holding the horses.

G

The range of rifle fire is 24 inches and hits are registered as follows:

At 24 inches to 12 inches—deduct *three* from every dice and remainder are hits. Thus 20 line infantry would fire four volleys at 24 inches, scoring 5, 4, 6, 1, which would mean 2 hits, 1 hit and 3 hits respectively.

At 6 inches to 12 inches—deduct *two*.

Under 6 inches—deduct *one*.

Cavalry are armed with carbines and their killing range is only 12 inches, at which distance 2 is deducted and 1 at 6-inch range. This applies if they are dismounted. If they are firing from the saddle then one more per dice has to be deducted, thus it is 3 from dice at 12 inches and 2 from dice at 6 inches.

Light troops have superior weapons and their range is extended to 30 inches, at which distance they deduct 3 from dice, at 18 inches they deduct 2 and 12 inches or under they deduct 1.

Odd numbers. If the firing troops do not exactly divide into their correct numbers, then divide as far as possible and all odd numbers work as follows—they fire individually and at maximum range have to throw a 6 on a dice (one dice per man), at middle range a 5 or 6 and at close range (6 inches) a 4, 5 or 6.

Deployment for firing. Troops may only fire their *front* rank, thus a unit formed up in threes will only fire its first rank, whereas the same unit deployed in single line will be able to have every man firing.

Troops situated on higher ground may fire over the heads of their own infantry if the terrain permits.

Troops making a double move *never* fire.

Covering fire. When a unit is moving into a hand-to-hand combat, adjacent friendly troops (within the limits of their rifle ranges) can fire on the enemy being attacked, thus giving covering fire to their own comrades.

Hand-to-hand fighting (*mêlées*)

A mêlée is deemed to have formed when one body of troops is brought into direct contact with another similar body of enemy troops. The attacker then declares that he has forced a mêlée and fighting takes place according to certain rules and conditions.

The writer assumes, quite reasonably it is thought, that hand-to-hand fighting, in which men use all their strength, cunning and skill to save their own lives whilst depriving the enemy of theirs, can be claimed to be much the same in any period. For that reason, fairly universal rules govern this facet of war gaming in the writer's circle—thus the conditions governing mêlées in this, the horse-and-musket period, are the same as those used in the Rules for Ancient Warfare, with the exception of the section governing the attack by cavalry or spearmen, which is inapplicable to this period (Section on Mêlées, Ancient Warfare, paragraph 2).

When assessing strengths for mêlée purposes, in this particular period all troops of Guards Regiments count as being *one* dice for every *four* men instead of five as with Light and Line units. This is an effort to reflect their higher morale and greater fighting power as picked troops.

SAVING THROWS OF DICE

In an effort to encourage aggression and to lessen the unrealistic speed with which troops were killed and taken from the battle, the 'Saving Throw of Dice' was instituted. It works in the following fashion:

Assume that 10 infantrymen have received hits in one move, the player to whom they belong throws simultaneously 10 dice. All dice that fall 5 or 6 represent men that have only been wounded and they are not removed from the battle but are allowed to remain on the table and continue to fight. All dice that throw below 5 or 6 indicate killed and that number of men are taken off the battlefield.

In view of the comparative importance of officers in the game, it is imperative to have some means of knowing whether it is an 'other rank' or an officer that has been killed. So, for every *five* dice that are thrown to save casualties, one coloured dice is added, that last dice representing the officer. Thus, with 10 casualties there would be eight white dice and two coloured dice.

When troops are under cover they add *one* to their saving throw, and officers *always* add one to theirs—thus a line infantryman behind a wall will be saved by a throw of 4, 5 or 6. An officer out in the open will be saved by a throw of 4, 5 or 6; the same officer behind a wall or dug-in can be saved by a dice throw of 3, 4, 5 or 6.

Cavalrymen are saved by a dice throw of 4, 5 or 6 as it is considered that some of the hits might well be upon the horse, which generally speaking is harder to kill than a man.

Houses, fortifications, etc.

Houses are graded in two classes—big and small; the big house can hold ten men and the small house five. These men need not actually be inside the house (which sometimes becomes confusing when mêlées take place) but may be stood or laid down behind it. Troops concealed in houses count as being under cover, they are not fired upon unless they fire first. When they are mêléed the fight takes place at the doorway, where one defender takes on one attacker with a straight dice throw deciding (defender adds one because he is under cover). If the defender wins, then another attacker can take his place next move, if the defender loses then the attacker is deemed to have entered the house where he takes on another defender, whilst another attacker fills the doorway. This goes on until the defenders have all been killed or the attackers ditto.

Troops attacking a house do so in the same way as they would if approaching a wall or other obstacle, they may be fired upon by defenders and may fire in return according to the ruling for this facet of the game.

At the commencement of the game a dice is thrown to find out from which direction the wind is blowing—1, north; 2, east; 3, north-west; 4, west; 5, south-east; 6, south. When a house or village comes under artillery or rifle fire, a dice is thrown at the start of *each* move to see if the house has caught fire. If a 1 or 2 is thrown it is on fire and must be evacuated by its occupants that move unless they wish to perish within it. In the case of a village the next house in the direction in which the wind is blowing will catch fire next move and so on until all houses from the original burning house in the same direction as the wind is blowing are alight. This does not mean that they cannot catch fire until so many moves elapse from the time when the original house caught fire, as a dice is thrown each move for *each* house under fire.

Troops may dig themselves in, or erect a barrier in one move, during this move they may not fire. If they are mêléed during their 'digging' move then they throw dice at only half the normal rate, as they are considered to have been caught semi-defenceless.

Forts or fortified houses. Attacking troops must not be laid out at start of game less than 2 ft. 6 in. from the fort.

Defending troops have unlimited rifle range—over 12 inches they deduct 3 from each dice (volleys of five men, etc., as in 'Firing' rules), at 6 inches to 12 inches deduct 2 and under 6 inches deduct 1.

Defending troops may move unlimited distances within the fort, thus reinforcements from one wall may get across to the other wall in one move regardless of the distance. Once the defenders leave the fort, however, in a sally for example, they move under normal move rates. They may only leave the fort at a recognized exit, such as a gate or sally-port, or an existing breach.

Attackers may attempt to enter a fort by means of ladders and over the walls, by knocking down the gates or by entering through a breach caused by artillery fire or by a mine. To enter via a ladder, two men must carry the ladder, and it takes 3 inches of their move to erect it against the wall. Three men may be on the ladder at one time, no attackers may move up to wall and then ascend ladder in same move—scaling ladder takes a complete move. Before move the defender throws a dice, and if he throws 5 or 6 he has succeeded in knocking ladder away from wall and all men on it must be thrown for (saving throws). Otherwise, a single man-to-man mêlée takes place exactly as in **house doorway.**

To knock down gates, a battering-ram may be carried up by five men in normal move distance (no double moves). It may not commence battering on the same move as it arrives at the gate, this operation takes a complete move. The ram cannot be operated by less than five men, a dice is thrown for each *two* men on the battering ram and their total score must beat the Defence Points Value of the gate, which is *ten*. Thus a ram with five men would throw two dice, if they scored two fives then they have knocked the gate down, if they had six men on the battering-ram they would throw three dice and, perhaps, throw 2, 3, 4—which would mean that the gate survives for that move.

A mine is placed in position under a wall by three men, who take a complete move to do so after arriving at the wall. They have two dice to score ten or more if they wish to blow a breach wide enough for two men abreast to pass through. They may continue to throw two dice as long as' there are at least three attackers standing by the mine.

Artillery may knock a breach in the walls by firing at the wall under normal rules for artillery firing—the wall has a points value of *ten* and the artillery can throw varying numbers of dice to attain this score, depending upon their distance from the wall, thus—at under 12 inches they throw *three* dice, between 12 inches and 24 inches they throw *two* dice. The breach caused by artillery fire is 3 inches in width.

HORSE-AND-MUSKET PERIOD:
'ACTION IN THE PLATTVILLE VALLEY'
24 July 1863

(American Civil War)

This was a small action between Federal and Confederate forces, each formed of three infantry brigades, one cavalry brigade and one battery of artillery—120 infantry, 30 cavalry, 2 guns each. It took place on a war-games table 8 feet by 5 feet in size, with hills made of plasticine, rivers and roads chalked in appropriate colours.

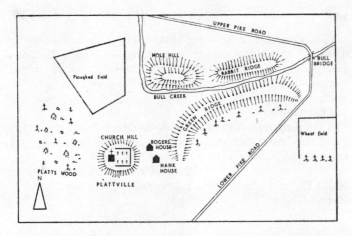

The battle lasted one full 'day' of eight game moves and actually took three and a half hours to play on the table.

Narrative
Both Federal and Confederate High Commands wish to control the small but important Plattville Valley and Village, each side sends a force to take over the area. The Federal force is commanded by General George H. Thomas and the Confederate force by General Jubal A. Early. Each side has an Advance Guard of one brigade (two infantry regiments) which, under the rules of this game, must move up the Upper and Lower Pike Roads respectively for the first move of the game—after this they may move in any desired direction. At the end of the third game move the remainder of each army arrives on its respective baseline and may come on to the table at any desired point.

THE ACTION

1st Game Move
The Federal Advance Guard, composed of Kearney's Brigade (10th Iowa and 2nd Illinois), move in a south-easterly direction along the Upper Pike Road, with 10th Iowa leading.

103

The Confederate Advance Guard move in a north-easterly direction along the Lower Pike Road—they are Pender's Brigade (7th Texas and 5th Kentucky) with the 7th Texas leading.

2nd Game Move

The 5th Kentucky turn north towards Green Ridge whilst the 7th Texas move further up the road before branching east towards the trees on the southern end of the Wheatfield.

Thd 10th Iowa carry on down the road towards the Bridge, whilst the 2nd Illinois turn southwards off the road towards Rabbit Ridge.

3rd Game Move

The 5th Kentucky form a skirmish line in the trees on the crest of the eastern half of Green Ridge, whilst the 7th Texas similarly form a firing line amongst the trees bordering the Wheatfield.

The 10th Iowa move over the Bridge towards the stone wall at the northern end of the Wheatfield, whilst the 2nd Illinois move on to Rabbit Ridge where they deploy along its crest.

At the conclusion of this move the remainder of the armies appear on their respective baselines.

4th Game Move

Confederates move forward from their baseline as follows:

2nd Virginia Cavalry towards Wheatfield.

1st Maryland and 6th Louisiana towards Green Ridge.

18th Georgia and 2nd Mississippi towards Village and Churchyard respectively.

1st North Carolina Cavalry towards Village.

1 gun with 2nd Virginia Cavalry to Wheatfield.

1 gun with 2nd Mississippi to Churchyard.

5th Kentucky and 7th Texas consolidate their firing lines on Green Ridge and southern end of Wheatfield respectively. Federals move forward from their baseline as follows:

PLATE 6

HORSE-AND-MUSKET BATTLE:
'ACTION IN THE PLATTVILLE VALLEY'

PLATE 7

PLATE 8

PLATE 9

PLATE 10

New York Fire Zouaves, Berdan's 1st U.S. Sharpshooters and 5th New Jersey move directly south on the Federal right flank immediately west of the Ploughed Field.

20th Maine move forward to Ploughed Field, over wall and cross plough.

4th Illinois Battery of Artillery move forward towards Mole Hill.

Grierson's 6th Illinois Cavalry and 1st Vermont Cavalry move forward to the shelter of the western end of Rabbit Ridge.

10th Iowa reach stone wall at northern border of Wheatfield and take up firing line in its shelter, with one company facing west towards end of Green Ridge.

2nd Illinois consolidate their position on Rabbit Ridge.

5th Game Move
Confederate move—left-flank gun moves into position in Churchyard. 2nd Mississippi move into Churchyard and into Church itself.

18th Georgia occupy the Rogers House and the Hank House (company in each), remainder of regiment deploy in village street.

1st Maryland and 6th Louisiana move on to Green Ridge, moving to extend line of 5th Kentucky, who turn a company to face the 10th Iowa on stone wall of Wheatfield.

1st North Carolina take up position under cover of Village.

2nd Virginia Cavalry charge forward over Wheatfield to attack 10th Iowa—they are supported by artillery and infantry fire from right-flank gun and 7th Texas.

Federal move—New York Fire Zouaves, Berdan's Sharpshooters and 5th New Jersey move forward towards northern end of Platts Wood.

20th Maine move forward across Ploughed Field.

Artillery get into position on Mold Hill.

1st Vermont Cavalry move towards Bridge.

2nd Illinois take part in fire-fight with Confederates on Green Ridge.

10th Iowa meet attack by Confederate cavalry on stone wall bordering Wheatfield.

Firing at end of 5th Game Move

(a) 1 company each of 10th Iowa and 5th Kentucky fire on each other at eastern end of Green Ridge and flank of stone wall by Wheatfield at 12-inch range.

10th Iowa (5 men)

1 dice—scores 3, thus 1 Confederate hit.

5th Kentucky (5 men)

1 dice—scores 4, thus 2 Federals hit.

Confederates' saving throw is 5, therefore no casualties.

Federal saving throw 3 and 4, thus 2 men killed.

(b) Remainder of 5th Kentucky (17 men) fire on Federals on Rabbit Ridge and 2nd Illinois fire back at 5th Kentucky. Thus:

5th Kentucky

17 men gives three volleys of 5 plus 2 men 'over'. Range 12 inches. So 1 dice per volley 3, 2, 2 (deduct 2 from each dice) means 1 hit. Odd men fire singly (must throw 5 or 6 at that range) but throw 4, 4. No hits. Therefore 2nd Illinois have 1 casualty—saving throw 6—no one killed.

2nd Illinois

10 men fire at 12-inch range—2 volleys. Throw 3, 2 = 1 hit.

10 men fire at 24-inch range—2 volleys. Throw 4, 4 = 2 hits.

Therefore 5th Kentucky have suffered 3 hits—saving throws save all three—no casualties.

(c) Federal artillery only in position this move, therefore are not eligible to fire.

(d) Confederate left-flank gun ditto.

(e) Confederate right-flank gun fires on 10th Iowa in support of 2nd Virginia Cavalry charge. Gun scores hit—throws two dice, scores 3, 2 = 5 hits on 10th Iowa, who throw saving throws and lose 2 men only.

(f) 7th Texas fire on 10th Iowa in support of cavalry charge. Texans have 20 men, so fire four volleys at 12-inch range. Throw 5, 6, 2, 3, thus score 8 hits. 10th Iowa save five so lose three.

(g) 10th Iowa (less 5 men killed) fire on attacking cavalry. Thus 10 men have 2 volleys—throw dice to ascertain range—5 thrown so range is 6 inches. Throw 6, 5 = 9 hits on cavalry. Cavalry save 4, so lose 5, including officer.

(h) Confederate infantry in Church (2 companies—10 men) —2nd Mississippi fire on 20th Maine in Ploughed Field. Also have 1 company in the Churchyard, so altogether fire 15 men or 3 volleys at 24-inch range. Throw 3, 3, 4 = 1 hit. 20th Maine saving throw loses them 1 man.

(i) 18th Georgia in Village—fire 3 volleys on 20th Maine at 24-inch range. Throw 5, 5, 4 = 5 hits. 20th Maine saving throws save 2 men, therefore 3 killed, including 1 officer.

(Note: Both 2nd Mississippi and 18th Georgia Regiments had full 20 men, but in each case only 15 men (or three volleys each) were actually in position to fire.)

Mêlée at end of 5th Game Move

Cavalry now reduced to 10 men after firing casualties face 10 men of 10th Iowa (regiment less 1 company of 5 men facing flankwards and 5 men killed).

Cavalry count 2 points per man, therefore they total 20 points. They do not get an impetus bonus for charging, as the infantry are behind a wall which reduces the shock effect of the charge. Infantry have ten men, so total 10 points.

Cavalry throw 4 dice (1 for each 5 points), 1, 2, 4, 3.

Infantry throw 2 dice, 6, 6.

Therefore cavalry have totalled 10, which gives them a score of 5 infantry killed. Infantry have totalled 12 points, which gives them 3 cavalry (6 points) killed.

Saving throws. Cavalry throw 4, 2, 2, so lose 2 men.
Infantry add 1 to saving throw because they are behind wall.

Throw 5, 5, 6, 5, 1, therefore infantry lose 1.

Thus, at end of first round of mêlée fighting: infantry have 9 men left on wall, cavalry have 8 men left.

Morale throw. As cavalry have lost their officer they have to throw dice to see state of their morale before fighting second round of mêlée. They throw 2, which means that they are 'shaken'. Throw again and throw 3, which means that they have to retreat one move in direction from which they came.

So, after one round of fighting, cavalry thrown back from wall, back through 7th Texas, this makes the infantry morale in question. 7th Texas throw dice, score 4, therefore morale is satisfactory and they remain steady.

End of 5th Game Move

This is the first game move of the battle in which anything important has happened and full details of this move can be seen in *Plates 6 and 7.*

In *Plate 6* (taken from behind Mole Hill, looking across Rabbit Ridge, Green Ridge towards Cornfield) 4th Illinois battery can be seen in the immediate foreground on Mole Hill with General Thomas and his staff beside the guns. To their left, on Rabbit Ridge, are the 2nd Illinois with the 6th Illinois Cavalry behind the ridge. On the immediate left flank can be seen the 1st Vermont Cavalry about to cross the Bridge as they go forward in support of 10th Iowa, who have just repelled the 2nd Virginia Cavalry at the stone wall bordering the Wheatfield—the cavalry can be seen turning away from the mêlée.

On Green Ridge the 5th Kentucky can be seen through the trees with their right flank turned and engaged in a fire-fight with the flank company of the 10th Iowa on the Wheatfield. Behind Green Ridge are the colours of the 1st Maryland and 6th Louisiana moving forward to the crest. The 7th Texas and the Confederate right-flank gun can be seen in the poplar trees at the far end of the Wheatfield.

Note piles of ammunition placed beside the guns.

In *Plate 7*, taken from behind the Confederate lines in Plattville Village and Church looking across at the Ploughed Field, with Platts Wood in the top left-hand corner of the plate, in the foreground are the 1st North Carolina Cavalry with the 18th Georgia occupying the Village in front of them. The left-hand gun of Peckham's Battery can be seen in the Churchyard with two companies of 2nd Mississippi, the other two companies being inside the Church.

Advancing across the Ploughed Field are the 20th Maine, whilst to their right can be seen the massed Federal flanking move, composed of the 5th New Jersey, then Berdan's Sharpshooters, with the New York Fire Zouaves hidden behind the trees of Platts Wood.

6th Game Move
Before movement takes place it is necessary for the 2nd Virginia Cavalry (who retreated last move from their mêlée) to see if their morale state has improved. They throw a dice—4, which means that they have rallied but remain stationary for this move.

Confederate Moves. 1 North Carolina Cavalry move in westerly direction behind shelter of Church Hill, facing southern end of Platts Wood.

1st Maryland and 6th Louisiana arrive on crest of Green Ridge and begin deploying.

5th Kentucky turn towards their right flank and present firing line towards 10th Iowa at Wheatfield stone wall.

Federal Moves. New York Fire Zouaves and Berdan's Sharp-shooters move forward on western side of Platts Wood, whilst 5th New Jersey advance through wood towards Church.

20th Maine line wall at southern end of Ploughed Field.

Artillery concentrates fire on Church and the Village.

2nd Illinois advance down forward slopes of Rabbit Ridge and move across Bull Creek towards Green Ridge.

1st Vermont Cavalry cross Bridge and advance down road until they halt behind 10th Iowa on stone wall.

Grierson's Illinois Cavalry remain behind west end of Rabbit Ridge.

Firing at end of 6th Game Move
Artillery. Confederate gun in Wheatfield fires on 10th Iowa—throws 1, which means *missed.*

Confederate gun in Churchyard—throws 5, which means a *hit.* Then throws 2, 3 = 5 hits on 20th Maine, who add 1 to their saving throw as they are in shelter of stone wall—they save 3, lose 2.

Federal Gun No. 1 firing on gun in Churchyard—throws 3, means a *hit.* Then throws 3, 4, which is insufficient to give a damaging hit on target.

Federal Gun No. 2 firing on troops in Village throws 4, which means a *hit.* Throws 2 dice—2, 3 = 5 hits on infantry, whose saving throw is plus 1 for shelter of houses—they save 2, lose 3.

Throw to see if house (Rogers House) has caught fire now that it is under fire—throw 4—no fire in house.

Rifle firing
(a) 7th Texas firing on 10th Iowa—4 volleys at 12 inches, 3, 1, 3, 1 = 2 hits. 10th Iowa saving throws—lose 2.

(b) 10th Iowa return fire—1 volley, 2 odd men at 12 inches, Dice 4: Odd men 3, 6 = 3 killed. 7th Texas saving throws—lose 1 man.

(c) 5th Kentucky on 10th Iowa—15 men can fire—3 volleys at 12 inches, 3, 3, 4=4 hit. 10th Iowa saving throw, 2 men killed.

(d) 10th Iowa return fire—1 volley at 12 inches, 6=4 hits. 5th Kentucky saving throws—2 men killed.

(e) 2nd Illinois firing on 5th Kentucky and 6th Louisiana—2 volleys on each at 12 inches, 3, 5, 6, 1=9 hits. Saving throws: 5th Kentucky lose 3 men, 6th Louisiana lose 1 officer and 1 man.

(f) 6th Louisiana can fire two volleys on 2nd Illinois at 12 inches, throw 3, 4=3 hits. 2nd Illinois saving throws—lose 1 man.

(g) 20th Maine firing on 2nd Mississippi in Churchyard—3 volleys at 12 inches, 3, 3, 6=6 hits. 2nd Mississippi saving throw—1 officer and 4 men lost.

(h) 2nd Mississippi firing on 20th Maine—4 volleys at 12 inches, 6, 5, 1, 1=7 hits. 20th Maine saving throw—5 men lost.

(i) 18th Georgia firing on 20th Maine—3 volleys at maximum range, 3, 3, 2=no hits.

End of 6th Game Move

7th Game Move

Before actual movement takes place it is necessary to see if the Church and the Rogers House are burning, as both have been under fire. Dice thrown for Church—4=no fire. Dice for Rogers House—3=no fire.

Confederate moves. 7th Texas leave shelter of trees on south border of Wheatfield and move across to attack 10th Iowa on the stone wall at northern end of Wheatfield. (10th Iowa now have only 6 men remaining to face this attack.)

The 8 remaining men of 2nd Virginia Cavalry move forward on to road immediately behind Green Ridge.

5th Kentucky turn 1 company (5 men) to face across valley where 2nd Illinois are attacking, remaining 2 companies (10 men) face east towards end of Green Ridge where they are attacked by 1st Vermont Cavalry.

1st Maryland deploy in trees on crest of Green Ridge to fight off attack by 2nd Illinois.

6th Louisiana form on their immediate left flank also on crest of Green Ridge, but facing partly towards Mole Hill and Ploughed Field.

1st North Carolina Cavalry move westwards and attack the flank of New York Fire Zouaves who have just come into view around southern end of Platts Wood.

Confederate infantry in Village and Churchyard hold their ground.

Federal moves. 1st Vermont Cavalry move towards eastern end of Green Ridge and charge up slopes to mêlée with part of 5th Kentucky facing them.

2nd Illinois charge up forward slope of Green Ridge and mêlée with remaining part of 5th Kentucky facing them and with 1st Maryland (who receive damaging covering fire from Federal artillery and advancing 2nd Illinois).

5th New Jersey advance through Platts Wood towards the Churchyard but still have not yet emerged from Wood.

Berdan's Sharpshooters, with New York Fire Zouaves on their immediate right flank come round southern end of Platts Wood, where the Zouaves expose their right flank, which is attacked by 1st North Carolina Cavalry moving from the cover of the Church Hill.

20th Maine remain under cover of stone wall in Ploughed Field from which they engage in fire-fight with 18th Georgia in Village.

Grierson's Illinois Cavalry remain under cover of Rabbit Ridge.

Firing at end of game move

Artillery. Confederate gun in Wheatfield firing on 10th Iowa. Throws 5=a *hit*. Then throws 3, 6=9 hits. 10th Iowa saving throw (plus 1 per dice because of shelter behind wall) saves 7, lose 2 men.

Confederate gun in Churchyard firing on Federal gun No. 1 on Mole Hill. Throws 4=a *hit*. Then throws 4, 5=9, which means that 2 of the crew of the Federal gun are killed so that gun cannot fire this move.

Federal gun No. 2 fires on 1st Maryland in support of 2nd Illinois attack—throws 6=a *hit*. Then throws 5, 3=8 hits. 1st Maryland saving throws (plus 1 for cover of trees) save 3, lose 5 men.

Rifle firing

(a) 7th Texas firing on 10th Iowa—4 volleys at 12 inches, 2, 2, 3, 1=1 hit. 10th Iowa saving throw—no casualties.

(b) 10th Iowa returning fire on 7th Texas—1 volley 1 single man 4: single man 5=3 hits. 7th Texas saving throw—2 men killed.

(c) 5th Kentucky firing on 1st Vermont Cavalry attacking them—2 volleys at 6 inches, 4, 2=4 hits. Cavalry saving throw —3 lost.

(d) 1st Maryland firing on 2nd Illinois attacking them—3 volleys at 6 inches, 4, 4, 3=8 hits. 2nd Illinois saving throw— 5 men lost.

(e) 1 company 5th Kentucky firing on 2nd Illinois attacking them—1 volley at 12 inches, 3=1 hit. 2nd Illinois saving throw —no loss.

(f) 6th Louisiana, firing two volleys on 2nd Illinois—1 volley at 6 inches, 3=2 hits. 1 volley at 12 inches, 5=3 hits. 2nd Illinois saving throw—3 men lost.

(g) 2nd Illinois firing as they attack on 1st Maryland—4 volleys at 6 inches, 6, 3, 4, 5=14 hits. 1st Maryland saving throw—2 officers, 8 men lost.

H

(h) 18th Georgia firing on 20th Maine—3 volleys and two odd men firing at long range (over 12 inches), 5, 1, 3 = 2 hits. Odd men 1, 4 = no hits. 20th Maine saving throw—1 man lost.

(i) 20th Maine firing in return on 18th Georgia—2 volleys at long range (over 12 inches), 5, 5 = 4 hits. 18th Georgia saving throw—3 men lost.

(j) 5th New Jersey firing from Platts Wood on Church— only 2 volleys possible—at long range, 3, 6 = 3 hits. 2nd Mississippi saving throw—2 men lost.

Mêlées

(i) 1st Vermont Cavalry (12 men) uphill against 10 men of 5th Kentucky on Green Ridge. 1st round of mêlée:

1st Vermont = 24 points (no impetus bonus becau se uphil charge).

5th Kentucky = 10 points.

1st Vermont throw 5 dice, 6, 5, 1, 1, 3 = 16, or 8 men hit.

5th Kentucky saving throw—lost 1 officer and 5 men. 5th Kentucky throw 2 dice, 6, 6 = 12 (6 points or 3 cavalry).

1st Vermont saving throw—lost 1 cavalryman. Cavalry now have 11 men left—infantry only 4; therefore 5th Kentucky are facing 'Overwhelming Numbers' and dice must be thrown for their morale. Dice thrown 6—so they fight on for second round of mêlée fighting.

1st Vermont—22 points = 4½ dice throws, 3, 4, 2, 5 + ½ of 2 = 15 points, or 8 infantrymen.

5th Kentucky—4 men = 1 dice—4 = 2 points or 1 cavalryman.

Saving throws: 1st Vermont lost 1 cavalryman.

5th Kentucky lost all remaining men.

Therefore at end of that mêlée 5th Kentucky (less 1 company in mêlée with 2nd Illinois) have been destroyed and 1st Vermont Cavalry (10 men remaining) have open flank facing them.

(ii) 2nd Illinois (13 men remaining) against 1st Maryland (7 men remaining) and 1 company 5th Kentucky (5 men).

1st Round
Each side throws two dice as they are approximately equal.

2nd Illinois, 5, 2=7=4 men hit.

1st Maryland/5th Kentucky, 5, 3=8=4 men hit.

Saving throws: 2nd Illinois—lost 3 men.

5th Kentucky—lost 1 man.

1st Maryland—lost 1 man.

2nd Round
2nd Illinois with 10 men has 2 dice, 3, 3=6=3 men hit.

5th Kentucky/1st Maryland with 10 men also have two dice throws, 4, 2=6=3 men hit.

Saving throws: 2nd Illinois—lost 1 man.

5th Kentucky—lost 1 man.

1st Maryland—lost 1 man.

Therefore at end of mêlée Confederates have 8 men remaining in this mêlée, whilst Federals have 9.

Morale throws: 2nd Illinois—4 remain in mêlée.

5th Kentucky/1st Maryland—5 remain in mêlée.

(iii) 1st North Carolina Cavalry hit New York Fire Zouaves in the flank. To ascertain what action the Zouaves take under these circumstances a dice must be thrown in accordance with the rule covering 'Flank Attacks'. Zouaves throw dice—3, this means that the whole unit retreats back 1 move (in good order and not routed), but every man in the unit has to be thrown for (saving throw) as though hit.

Zouaves' saving throw—lost 1 officer and 9 men.

As a unit on its immediate flank has broken, Berdan's Sharpshooters must now dice to see how its own morale stands—throws 2, which means that it is 'shaken', but second throw of 5 causes the unit to be rallied.

End of 7th Game Move

Plate 8 shows the Confederate left flank in the area of Plattville Village and the Churchyard. 18th Georgia are still defending the Village, although depleted in numbers, as are the 2nd Mississippi in the Church and the Churchyard.

On the left can be seen the 1st North Carolina Cavalry charging home in their flank attack on the New York Fire Zouaves, behind whom can be seen Berdan's Sharpshooters. Masked by the Church, part of 5th New Jersey can be seen emerging from Platts Wood, whilst on the right of the picture the end file of 20th Maine can be seen firing over the stone wall of the ploughed field.

8th Game Move

The last move before nightfall. Dice thrown for Church and Rogers House to see if they are on fire—both not yet burning.

Confederate moves. 7th Texas move forward and engage remnants of 10th Iowa on stone wall at end of Wheatfield.

2nd Virginia Cavalry (8 men) move forward and engage in mêlée with 1st Vermont Cavalry (10 men).

1st North Carolina Cavalry, after taking heavy losses from Federal right-flank units, move back into shelter of Church Hill.

18th Georgia leave village and move into Churchyard to reinforce 2nd Mississippi who have had losses.

6th Louisiana move towards their right and are engaged by Grierson's Illinois Cavalry who come across Creek from behind Rabbit Ridge.

Federal moves. 10th Iowa engage in mêlée with 7th Texas. 2nd Illinois remain in mêlée on Green Ridge. Grierson's Illinois Cavalry move forward from shelter of Rabbit Ridge, across Creek and up slope of Green Ridge where they mêlée with 6th Louisiana on crest of Ridge.

20th Maine (2 officers and 6 men) leave shelter of wall on Ploughed Field and advance towards Village.

5th New Jersey move forward to foot of west slopes of Church Hill.

Berdan's Sharpshooters, followed by remnants of New York Fire Zouaves, move towards foot of Church Hill alongside 5th New Jersey.

Firing at end of 7th Game Move
Artillery. Federal Gun No. 1 firing on Confederate gun in Churchyard—range 2 feet to 3 feet. Throws 5—a *hit*. Throws two dice, 6, 6, which means that Confederate gun and crew are all destroyed.

Federal Gun No. 2 cannot fire this move as it lost two of its crew last move.

Confederate gun at Wheatfield fires on 1st Vermont Cavalry to support charge of 2nd Virginia Cavalry. Range 1 foot to 2 feet—throws 4=a *hit*. Throws two more dice, 3, 1=4 cavalry hit. 1st Vermont saving throw=2 men killed.

Rifle fire
　(a) 10 Iowa firing on 7th Texas attacking them—6 men at 6 inches—1 volley, 5 and 1 odd man throws 4=5 hits. 7th Texas saving throw=4 men lost.

　(b) 7th Texas firing at 12 inches range on 12 Iowa (range decided by dice)—3 volleys and 2 odd men=4, 4, 2 and odd men 1, 3=2 hits. 10th Iowa saving throw=1 man lost.

　(c) 6 men of 18th Georgia firing on 20th Maine at long range—3; odd man 1=no hits.

　(d) 10 men of 18th Georgia (in Churchyard) firing on 20th Maine at long range—two volleys—4, 4=2 hits. 20th Maine saving throw=2 men lost.

　(e) 20th Maine firing on 18th Georgia on hill—8 men at

long range = 1 volley, 5 plus 3 odd men, 6, 3, 3 = 3 hits. 18th Georgia saving throw = 3 men lost.

(f) 5th New Jersey firing on Church and 2nd Mississippi in Churchyard—2 volleys on Church at 6 inches, 3, 6 = 7 hits.

2 volleys on 2nd Mississippi in yard, 3, 4 = 5 hits.

2nd Mississippi saving throw—5 men lost.

(g) 2nd Mississippi—18 men in Church and Churchyard firing on 5th New Jersey at 6-inch range. 3 volleys, 5, 4, 2, plus 3 odd men who score 4, 4, 1 = 10 hits. 5th New Jersey saving throw = 1 officer and 5 men lost.

(h) New York Fire Zouaves firing on A Squadron 1st North Carolina Cavalry (5 men) who are attacking them.

11 men fire at 6-inch range—2 volleys—3, 4, plus 1 odd man who scores 4—thus 6 cavalry are hit. 1st North Carolina Cavalry saving throw—3 men lost.

(Before (h) actually took place, the 1st North Carolina Cavalry had split into two (A Squadron of 5 men and B/C Squadrons of 10 men) and had charged against the New York Fire Zouaves and Berdan's Sharpshooters respectively. As both these infantry formations were formed up in double rank, the cavalry had to throw a dice to see if they charged home. A squadron of the cavalry threw 5 so they charged home, suffering casualties from firing as shown in (h) above. B/C Squadrons threw 2 so did *not* charge home, the necessary second dice thrown was a 1 which caused the cavalry to swerve *right* for another 12 inches, which was the remainder of their move distance, during this they were fired upon as under.)

(i) Berdan's Sharpshooters fire on B/C Squadrons 1st North Carolina Cavalry (front ranks only fire) 2 volleys at 6 inches range, 5, 2 = 5 hits. 1st North Carolina saving throw—lost 1 officer and 3 men.

Mêlées at end of 7th Game Move
1st round
7th Texas on 10th Iowa in Wheatfield; 7th Texas (16 men) no

impetus bonus because 10th Iowa are behind stone wall. 3 dice = 4, 3, 3 = 10, or 5 men hit.

10th Iowa (5 men) 1 dice, 6 = 3 men.

Saving throws: 7th Texas lose 3 men.

10th Iowa lose 1 man.

Therefore, at end of 1st round of fighting 7th Texas have 13 men and 10th Iowa have 4 men. 7th Texas are therefore in 'Overwhelming Numbers' so 10th Iowas must dice to see what happens to them—dice throw 1—all remaining men of 10th Iowa are cut down. 7th Texas are left in possession of stone wall at north end of Wheatfield.

2nd Virginia Cavalry against 1st Vermont Cavalry in rear of eastern end of Green Ridge.

2nd Virginia Cavalry have 8 men and add 1 to each dice for impetus bonus, thus they throw 2 dice, 3, 4 plus 2 = 9, or 5 cavalry.

1st Vermont Cavalry have 8 men and throw 2 dice, 6, 4 = 10 or 5 cavalry.

Saving throws: 2nd Virginia Cavalry lose 3 men.

1st Vermont Cavalry lose 2 men.

2nd round of fighting

2nd Virginia Cavalry 5 men—1 dice, 2 = 1 man hit.

1st Vermont Cavalry 6 men—1 dice, 6 = 3 men hit.

Saving throws: 2nd Virginia Cavalry lose 3 men.

1st Vermont Cavalry lose 1 man.

Therefore at end of both rounds of fighting the 2nd Virginia Cavalry are left with 2 men and the 1st Vermont Cavalry are left with 5 men—therefore 'Overwhelming Numbers' rule applies and 2nd Virginia Cavalry throw dice—throw 4 which means that they surrender if no supporting troops are within one infantry move of them. But as the 7th Texas are within that distance then 2nd Virginia Cavalry must retreat one move.

Throw dice to see if retreat is orderly or a rout—5 thrown so orderly move. Thus 1st Vermont Cavalry are left in possession of mêlée area.

Mêlée on Green Ridge (continued from last game move)
2nd Illinois have 9 men left and 1st Maryland have 4 men.

The mêlée is joined by 5 men of 5th Kentucky on right flank of 1st Maryland and by 6th Louisiana (2 officers and 19 men) on left flank of 1st Maryland.

Grierson's Illinois Cavalry come from behind Rabbit Ridge, over Bull Creek, and charge into 6th Louisiana.

(None of these new arrivals in the already-established mêlée gets any impetus bonus as it is not a newly formed mêlée.) Therefore one large mêlée is constituted composed of 9 infantry and 15 cavalry of the Federal Force and 30 Confederate infantry. With infantry counting 1 point and cavalry 2 points the strengths are as follows:

Federals have 39 points. Confederates have 30 points. Federals throw 8 dice, 6, 1, 4, 2, 1, 5, 5, 6 = 30 or 15 men hit. Confederates throw 6 dice, 2, 2, 3, 6, 1, 1 = 15 or 8 points hit.

> *Saving throws:* Federals 3 cavalry (6 points) and 2 infantry thrown for—losses are 1 cavalryman and 2 infantrymen.
>
> Confederates throw for 15 infantry and lose 2 officers and 9 men.

2nd round
Federals have 14 cavalry (28 points) and 7 infantry (7 points), total of 35 points—7 dice, 3, 3, 5, 5, 5, 2, 2 = 25 or 13 hit.

Confederates have 19 points—4 dice, 6, 6, 4, 3 = 19, or 10 points hit.

> *Saving throws:* Federals throw for 4 cavalry (8 points) and 2 infantry (2 points)—losses are 3 cavalry and 1 infantry killed.
>
> Confederates throw for 10 infantry and lose 1 officer and 6 infantry.

Total remaining forces at end of both mêlée rounds:

Federals: 11 cavalry and 6 infantry.
Confederates: 12 infantry.

Morale dice throws: Federals throw 4 so are O.K.

Confederates throw 2 which means they are 'shaken', second dice throw is 4—so they all retreat 1 move, facing enemy.

2 Cavalrymen of 1st North Carolina Cavalry attack New York Fire Zouaves at southern end of Platts Wood.

1st round

Cavalry 4 points—1 dice—3 plus 1 for impetus bonus = 4 or 2 infantry hit.

Zouaves have 8 infantry in front rank—2 dice, 4, 4 = 8, or 4 points.

Saving throws: Federals lose 2 infantry.
Confederates lose 1 cavalryman.

Thus, remaining are 11 Federal infantry and 1 Confederate cavalryman, who is faced by 'Overwhelming Numbers'—he throws a 1 on the dice and is therefore cut down.

End of 8th Game Move and nightfall

The situation at the conclusion of the 8th Game Move, as dusk descends, is clearly shown in *Plates 9 and 10. Plate 9* is looking from behind the Federal lines, across Mole Hill and Green Ridge towards the Wheatfield. On Green Ridge can be seen Grierson's Illinois Cavalry and survivors of 2nd Illinois Infantry—on their left flank are remainder of 1st Vermont Cavalry coming up eastern slope of Ridge to join them. In the background are the 7th Texas by the stone wall they have just wrested from 10th Iowa. In the background can be seen the survivors of 5th Kentucky Infantry and 2nd Virginia Cavalry beyond Pike Road, whilst remnants of 1st Maryland and 6th Louisiana move down the rear slopes of the Ridge. 4th

Illinois Artillery, General Thomas and his staff can be seen on Mole Hill in foreground, with artillery limbers behind hill.

In *Plate 10* the view is from directly behind the Confederate lines in the Churchyard on their left flank of the battle. The survivors of 1st North Carolina Cavalry are in the immediate foreground with 18th Georgia and 2nd Mississippi in Churchyard and (out of sight) in Church itself. The wrecked gun can be seen in the corner of the Churchyard. On the left of the picture can be seen Berdan's Sharpshooters advancing towards the Church with remainder of New York Fire Zouaves immediately behind them. Partly masked by the Church are 5th New Jersey and, in the space between the Church Hill and the Ploughed Field, the survivors of 20th Maine are moving forward. In the right background can be seen Mole Hill with the Federal artillery in position.

Moves after nightfall
The Confederate forces in the Churchyard area, seeing their line of retreat being possibly cut, withdraw under cover of darkness, joining their right-wing survivors on the Lower Pike Road.

The Federals, being left in possession of Plattville, have achieved their objective and secured the Valley.

(The troops used in this battle belong to the author—they consist of many different makes and include in the actual photographs the following: S.A.E., Scruby (both original and conversions), Spencer-Smith plastic figures, gun limbers by Ed Saunders, cannon by John Hatherway of U.S.A., a large number of home-cast figures and conversions—the standard bearers, for example, mostly being German infantry of World War II converted into Civil War figures by the addition of rolled blankets around their bodies, slouch hats or kepis instead of steel helmets, etc. Some trees are home-made and on the Ridge they are Lone Star tree kits, the bridges are home-made, the houses and church are Triang rubber models, the log fence is cast in plaster of Paris in a rubber mould, model-railway scenery can be seen lining each baseline, the hills, of course, are plasticine built up on shaped pieces of wood.)

8

Modern Warfare

TANK AND INFANTRY ACTION ON THE ST JAMES ROAD

BEFORE proceeding with this chapter on modern war games it is felt that some explanatory notes are required, particularly as there are two sets of rules for this period as against one set only for other periods mentioned.

The second rather sparse and comparatively simple set of rules given in this chapter were originally the only rules the author intended to use to cover modern warfare. However, in Bristol there lives a fanatically enthusiastic war gamer—Lionel Tarr—who specializes in modern games and has been re-fighting the German attack on Russia of 1941 for at least the past four years. When last visited Tarr was calmly building a scaled-down representation of Stalingrad because that was the point at which his war had arrived.

During the course of that same visit the author was given the opportunity of actually witnessing Tarr fight one of his battles; this was possible because Tarr fights 'solo' against himself. Most war gamers fight in this manner because they are unable to find an opponent but Lionel Tarr prefers it this way and for the type of warfare he is fighting this is perhaps the best method. At one stage he was involved in a postal war game in which he received tactical instructions for the movement of German troops from a serving soldier in Aden. Although thousands of miles apart a reasonably satisfactory war game resulted.

The game played to Tarr's rules assumes a realism far in advance of most known war games, and, although the rules might at first appear highly complicated, they become easy on further acquaintance and cover almost every conceivable facet of modern war games. For example, many of the artillery 'shoots' are done with maps, the actual guns not even being on the war-games table, but their fire is directed by an observer actually hidden on the table and the guns fire on one of the many large-scale maps of the terrain tacked to the wall. Aircraft, both fighters and bombers, actually come into the battle —they are models scaled to the correct size that fly over the table to a movement scale laid down in the rules; they are supported on a close-mesh twine netting suspended over the table, although now it is believed that Tarr has got a large sheet of transparent plastic stretched on a frame over the table. Paratroop drops also take place in the same way. The aircraft set off from airfields marked on maps and can be bombed by enemy aircraft if within range.

So impressive are the results obtained when using Tarr's rules that the author was delighted to receive permission to include them herewith in their entirety, representing as they do a very fine, realistic set of rules for modern warfare.

LIONEL TARR'S RULES

Preliminary Action. Before fighting the actual war game, all forces move on a map, gridded into a number of squares and scaled one inch on the map to one foot on the war-games table—thus each square equals one 'table'. When two opposing forces enter a map square this action is transferred to the war-games table. Whilst the game is actually taking place on the table, other map moves can take place until forces of equal strength enter another table area when one puts the other in 'check'.

The terrain made on the table for the actual game reproduces, of course, all the salient features such as hills, roads, rivers, etc., shown on the actual map square.

Moves. Each player throws a dice to decide who moves first for each game move.

Move Distances

Arm	Road inches	Cross-country inches	Arm	Road inches	Cross-country inches
Infantry	5	4	Self-propelled guns	8	8
Cavalry	10	8	Jag Panther tank	8	8
Horse artillery	8	6	Fighter aircraft	36	6 moves over table
Horse transport	8	6			
Motor transport	24	18	Tactical aircraft	24	5 moves over table
Half-tracks	24	24			
Light armour	18	18	Heavy bomber	24	8 moves over table
Spotter planes	18	10 moves over table			
			Transports	24	8 moves over table
Medium tank	10	10			
Heavy tank	8	8			

Firing

Ranges

Weapon	Killing Range inches	Weapon	Killing Range inches inches
Sub-machine gun	3	88 mm field gun	60 HE 36 AP
Flame (man-pack)	3	88 mm a/aircraft	40
Flame (tank)	6	105 S.P. gun	80 HE 50 AP
A/tank projector	6	122 S.P. gun	100 HE 60 AP
Rifle	12	75 mm field gun	60 HE 30 AP
Light machine.gun	15	3.7 cm armd. car gun	22
Heavy machine gun	18	75 mm tank gun	30 AP 60 HE
15/20 mm cannon	18	88 mm tank gun	36 AP 60 HE
5 cm mortar	1½ to 9	76 mm tank gun	30 AP 60 HE
8 cm mortar	6 to 24	85 mm tank gun	36 AP 60 HE
12 cm mortar	6 to 60	82 mm recoilless a/tank	
45 mm a/tank gun	25	gun	30 AP
Twin-barrelled heavy machine gun, dive-bombers or ground strafing	18		

Calculation of casualties (small arms). 6 rifles or 3 sub-machine guns; 1 light m/g; 1 heavy m/g or 1 mortar bomb equal one dice and the number scored on that dice is the number of hits scored if target is in open. Troops under cover in buildings, trenches, woods, etc., only suffer quarter-rate (except if mortar fire when it is half-rate). When opposing forces meet, each throws a dice and the highest has the right to fire first. This is excepted in the case of flanking (enfilade) fire which always take precedence. Troops enfiladed thus are always subjected to *two* volleys before being able to return the fire.

Artillery firing (including mortars). This kind of fire-power can come under one of three headings:

        1. Open sight firing.

        2. Observed firing.

        3. Map firing.

For complete control and to obtain results that most resemble reality the following conditions apply:

1. *Open sight firing.* In cases where the target is visible from the site of the gun or mortar—fire for effect of hit by using burst-circle or points system to determine casualties (see below).

2. *Observed fire.* An observer must be in a position where he can see the target and he will direct the guns on to the target (as the gunners are not in a position to see it for themselves). One dice is thrown for each gun to decide the range and a 5 or 6 is necessary to obtain that range. If, however, one observer is observing for more than one gun, only one gun of that group needs to range to enable *all* guns of that group to fire. If that observer is killed, of course, *all* guns have lost range instead of only one gun if he were only observing for that one.

When the target is one specific object such as a house or a machine-gun post the dice now thrown to see effect of fire also has to be a 5 or 6 for a direct hit. If lower number is scored the object at which gun is aimed has been missed by 6 inches and a burst-pattern placed over point of impact decides casualties.

3. *Map firing.* Observers are not required for this type of fire which is directed by Gun Position Officers on to unseen areas (that is, areas unseen by these officers). This is mainly used for harassing only, but should the area concerned contain troops, vehicles, stores, etc., losses can probably be inflicted. Ranging rounds have to be thrown as in Section 2 above, but a further 6 is required to hit a specific objective or to inflict losses in men. If less than 6 is scored use burst-pattern as above.

Targets ranged. It is necessary only to range a target or area once from any one gun position, as weapons once ranged can switch targets accurately. But should a gun be moved then ranging rounds must be fired again. Similarly, a switch right or left, and an increase or decrease in range, can be made without a ranging round.

Burst-pattern. This is a circle of card or perspex of a specified diameter (according to weapon concerned) which is placed over point of impact when hit is scored. Everything or everyone within that circle is considered hit. Sizes of circles are as follows: 75 mm: 3 inches; 88 mm: 4 inches; 105 mm: 5 inches; 50 mm mortar: 3 inches; 80 mm mortar: 3 inches; 120 mm mortar: 4 inches; tactical bomb: 5 inches; heavy bomb: 6 inches; anti-personnel mine: 3 inches.

Material damage. To determine material damage the following points system is used: All weapons have a *strike points value* depending upon their calibre or power and all appropriate material has a *defence points value*, based on strength and speed of moving vehicle, for example. To decide whether a hit has been scored, three dice are thrown by firer simultaneously, their total score *plus* the particular weapon's *Strike Points Value* must equal or exceed the *Defence Points Value* to destroy that objective. (Thus, an 88 mm Field Artillery piece with a strike points value of 5 is trying to hit a reinforced blockhouse with a defence points value of 18. The firer throws his three dice and scores 5, 5 and 3—a total of 13 plus his 5 strike value gives him 18 also—thus the blockhouse is hit and destroyed.)

Individual targets attacked from the air carry a maximum points value of 20, but a town, as a whole, has only its normal defence value.

Weapon/machine	Strike	Defence
Infantry a/tank rifle	3	—
Inf. a/tank rocket projector	6	—
Inf. a/tank gun 3.7:4.5	4	15
Inf. a/tank gun 88 mm	5	15
Field artillery 7.2	4	13
Field artillery 8.8	5	13
* Self-propelled gun 7.5	4	14
* Pzkw III tank 7.5 gun	4	14
* Pzkw V tank 8.8 gun	5	16
* T34 tank 76 mm gun	4	15
* T34 tank 85 mm gun	5	16
* T60 tank 45 mm gun	3	14
* Self-propelled gun 8.8 cm	5	15
* Self-propelled gun 122 mm	6	15
* Armoured car 3.7 cm	3	13
Fighter aircraft	6	22
Tactical bomber	6	20
Medium/heavy bomber	10	22
† Twin-barrel A/A cannon	4	—
A/tank mine	6	
A/personnel mine	as per burst-pattern	
(1 dice is thrown each move per tank or man whilst on the minefield. 5, 6 means hit and further dice are thrown to discover effect.)		
Soft vehicles (lorries etc.)	—	7
Buildings	—	7
Reinforced blockhouses	According to weapons therein	18

* All armoured vehicles have defence points for their thicker frontal armour when hit (plus 2 points). They lose 2 points when hit on the side and lose 3 points when hit in rear.

† Can engage aircraft which is ground-strafing.

Air strikes. Individual targets attacked from the air carry a defence points value of 20—a dice throw that scores below this figure means a miss of 6 inches and a burst-pattern is used to ascertain casualties. Troops inside buildings hit by bombs are considered killed. Troops shot-up from the air suffer normal casualties.

Flame-throwers. When used against infantry equals one sub-machine gun. When ranged upon tank from rear and within its specified range it takes a strike points value of 6. When used against houses, the house is automatically 'fired' and troops within have dice thrown for them as usual. Any survivors retire via the opposite side of the house to that from which the attack came—if this is not possible, then all survivors are also destroyed.

Mines. Minefields are marked upon the map of the player who has them. They are laid by engineering troops with each man laying 1 inch to each side of himself and he moves at a quarter of his normal rate. Personnel thus engaged are non-combatants but are armed to defend themselves if they are attacked. There are two types of mines—anti-tank and anti-personnel. Anti-tank have a strike points value of 6 per tank for as long as the tank is actually on the minefield. Anti-personnel mines have a burst-pattern as ruled and a dice is thrown each move for as long as the troops are on the minefield. Troops who do not move are safe. All vehicles and troops crossing minefields only move at half their normal rate.

Smoke. All burning material produces smoke. A smoke canister fired by a tank, for example, produces smoke for a distance of 6 inches from where the canister lands. A tank or building that is on fire produces smoke for a distance of 9 inches. This smoke is represented by coloured cotton wool about 6 inches in height and it lasts for a specific number of moves depending upon wind strength. At commencement of battle throw dice to determine wind strength (see below). If wind is *slow* smoke remains in position for 4 moves, if wind is *medium* for 3 moves, and if wind is *fast* for only 2 moves.

Wind dice throw: 1 or 2 means from north, 3 means south, 4 means east and 5 or 6 means west. Dice for strength: 1/2, slow; 3/4, medium; 5/6, strong.

I

Hand-to-hand fighting. When troops come into actual contact in this fashion, one dice per six men involved is thrown. Casualties are half dice score. This procedure continues until one of the two forces is at half its original strength, then morale rule (see below) applies. If men stand fast, mêlée continues under same conditions.

Morale. When half the number of men attacked are killed, a dice has to be thrown to determine the morale of the remainder. 1 or 2=men stand fast, 3 or 4=an orderly withdrawal and 5 or 6=routed. When troops are routed they move at double their normal rate until baseline or friendly troops are reached (whichever is nearest). Mechanical vehicles move at normal rate.

Concealment. When troops or equipment are in positions out of sight of enemy they need not be placed upon the table but must be noted upon their commander's map. Night movements are similarly concealed and take place in *one* move which incorporates all the eight moves of darkness. The periscope (see separate note) must be used at all times to obtain vision from the actual model height on to all troops, vehicles, etc., possibly hidden by undulating ground, trees, etc. Such troops (excepting gunners and mortarmen) cannot fire and remain concealed unless sniping is carried out.

Day/night. Daylight is deemed to be the first 14 moves of the game; night is the next 10 moves—the whole equals 24 hours, or one day.

Paratroops. The use of paratroops or glider-borne troops is subject to the following conditions:

1. 18 men per aircraft.

2. 1 piece of equipment (i.e. gun and limber, light truck and crew, etc.) per glider.

3. Paratroops land on Dropping Zone and gliders on Landing Zone en masse and not deployed. They cannot fire

whilst dropping, and dropping itself counts as one move. Para transports when hit by flak are brought down and one dice is thrown for every six men on board—the number thrown represents paratroops who are uninjured and bale out as per Condition 3 above. Gliders hit and brought down also include troops not fitted with parachutes.

Motorized infantry. When vehicles containing troops are attacked, first use points system to determine if lorry is hit and destroyed then carry on in same way as for paratroopers in plane hit by flak (see above).

Barbed wire. Dannert Wire is laid by two men in normal moves. Wire halts infantry one move and it can be crushed flat by tank making pathway same width as tank for infantry to pass through.

Trenches and foxholes. Troops digging these can take *two* moves to dig a trench big enough for their personal use.

Street fighting. Assaulting infantry can cross a street in their normal move but must split it into two thus—if their move is 5 inches then they move 2½ inches, halt for firing (their own and enemy) and then survivors carry on remaining 2½ inches. This is to give defenders chance to fire. Defending forces suffer half casualties when under rifle fire, and two-thirds casualties when under heavier fire such as machine guns. Mortar fire gives one-quarter casualties.

Visibility. At commencement of battle throw dice for wind (already covered) and for visibility. These situations decided by dice prevail throughout that particular battle. Dice throw of 1/2 means rainy, overcast conditions; throw of 3/4 means normal conditions; throw of 5/6 means bright, sunny day. If rainy and overcast, throw dice again. 1/2 means visibility of 28 inches, 3/4 visibility 34 inches, 5/6 means visibility of 60 inches.

Bombers hit. When loaded up and hit, a bomber can either blow up or jettison its load. One dice decides 1–3 it jettisons and 4–6 it blows up. When jettisoning—if by a Stuka the bomb is dropped immediately under where plane is hit, if by medium/ heavy bomber bombs drop in line directly along route of aircraft. To decide position, a marker is dropped from bomb-bay under plane, from point where this marker touches ground measure 8 inches and this is the position of last bomb, casualties decided by dice and burst-pattern based on strike value.

Final assessment. If the battle is part of a campaign, at end of game count casualties both in vehicles, artillery and men. They are then divided accordingly: one-third of them are totally destroyed and out for good, one-third are considered hospitalized and recover in 6 moves from end of game, whilst one-third are replaced by reserves who join main body in three moves from end of battle.

A SIMPLIFIED SET OF RULES FOR MODERN WAR GAMES

The Move:

Infantry	6	inches
Motorized transport	12	,,
Tanks	18	,,
Armoured cars	18	,,
Half-tracks	15	,,
Scout cars	18	,,
Guns (unlimbered)	6	,,
Guns (limbered)	12	,,

Guns may move half distance and fire. Limbering/unlimbering takes 3 inches. 3 inches bonus for all arms on roads. Half-rate up opposed hills.

Firing:

Flame-thrower, SMG. and Bazooka	6	inches
Rifle and LMG	12	,,

| Mortar | not less than 18 inches |
| | and not more than 36 ,, |

88 mm, 75 mm, 25 pdr., tank gun: unlimited range depending upon obstacles within field of fire.

Anti-tank gun	36 ,,
Tank machine gun	24 ,,
Armoured-car gun (2 pdr)	24 ,,

To score a hit, throw dice: 4, 5 or 6 scores a hit for anti-tank
guns or 2 pdrs. 3, 4, 5 or 6 scores hit for 88 mm, 75 mm, 25
pdr, tank gun and mortar.

Casualties:
Tanks (can only be knocked out by 88mm, 75 mm, 25 pdr,
anti-tank gun):

Throw 2 dice. Total 12—knocked out

11   ,,

10   ,,   2 moves

9   ,,   1 move

If tank is 'hull down' then deduct *one* from score.

Armoured cars (by 88 mm, 75 mm, 25 pdr):

Total 9, 10, 11 or 12—knocked out

8   ,,   2 moves

7   ,,   1 move

If fired upon by 2 pdr deduct 1 from dice total.

Scout car or half-track (tank, 88 mm, 75 mm, 25 pdr, anti-
tank, mortar, 2 pdr):

2 dice:

Total 8, 9, 10, 11 or 12—knocked out (occupants killed)

7—out for 2 moves

6—out for 1 move

Soft vehicle (by tank, 88 mm, 75 mm, 25 pdr, anti-tank,
mortar, 2 pdr):

7, 8, 9, 10, 11 or 12—knocked out (occupants killed)

6—knocked out for 2 moves

5—knocked out for 1 move

If shot up by machine gun add *two* to dice score.

Guns (by tank, 88 mm, 75 mm, 25 pdr, mortar):

10, 11, 12—knocked out

9   ,,   2 moves

8   ,,   1 move

If by 2 pdr deduct *one* from dice score.

Personnel:

LMG, 2 pdr—throw 1 dice, full score counts as hits.

Mortar, 88 mm, 75 mm, 25 pdr, tank gun—throw $1\frac{1}{2}$ dice, full score counts as hits.

SMG—1 dice, half score counts as hits.

Rifles—1 dice per volley of five men, deduct 3 at range between 12 inches and 24 inches, deduct 2 range 6 inches to 12 inches, deduct 1 range under 6 inches.

Saving throws. All personnel count only as wounded and may stay in game if dice throw scores 5 or 6 for them (one dice being thrown per casualty). If under cover 4, 5 or 6 counts.

Flamethrower. 6-inch range—dice thrown and 1 deducted from score. No saving throws. Remainder within 6-inch radius throw dice for morale.

Morale. As in Horse-and-Musket rules.

Mêlées. As in Horse-and-Musket rules.

WORLD WAR II

'TANK AND INFANTRY ACTION ON THE ST JAMES ROAD'

Figures

Airfix OO gauge British and German infantry (plastic).

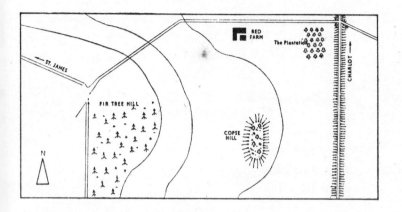

Roskopf OO gauge mortar teams, machine gunners and artillery observers (plastic).

Authenticast anti-tank-gun teams (metal).

Home-cast mortar teams, machine gunners, anti-tank guns.

Vehicles

Airfix Sherman tanks (plastic).

Home-made plaster-of-Paris German tanks.

Britains' OO gauge lorries.

Lesney 'Matchbox' series military vehicles.

Terrain

Sandtable 6 ft × 3 ft—battle fought lengthways.

Trees: Lone Star plastic kits; also home-made.

House: Home-made.

Narrative

1st Battalion Grenadier Guards, supported by A Squadron, 3rd Royal Tank Regiment, are holding the high ground covering the St James Road. This town is a vital centre of communications and must be held.

The Hermann Goering Panzer Grenadiers will attack over the Charlot Road Embankment.

Strength of forces is as follows:

British
1st Battalion Grenadier Guards
   HQ, A, B, C, Companies (10 men each).

   2 mortars.

   3 anti-tank guns.

   3 machine guns.

   3 Sherman tanks.

Germans
Hermann Goering Panzer Grenadiers
   2 regiments motorized infantry (30 men each).

   3 half-tracked vehicles.

   3 personnel-carrying trucks.

   6 Panther tanks.

   3 mortars.

   2 anti-tank guns.

   3 machine guns.

This action was fought under the simplified rules for modern warfare given earlier in this book. It could equally well, and probably more realistically, have been fought under Lionel Tarr's excellent rules. It is intended to describe it by giving photographs of the action at its more significant points, with explanatory notes on the plates.

Plate 11—The Opening Dispositions
The action consisted of an attack by German forces initially off the table against British troops and armour in prepared positions. This plate shows the British forces as they were placed and German forces as they came on to the field on their first move.

PLATE 11

MODERN BATTLE: 'TANK AND INFANTRY ACTION
ON THE ST JAMES ROAD'

PLATE 12

PLATE 13

PLATE 14

PLATE 15

Looking from behind the British positions, in the immediate foreground is the eastern edge of the wood on Fir Tree Hill. In front and to the right are the HQ Company of the Guards, in reserve, with an anti-tank gun and a machine gun. To their left, behind a belt of barbed wire, lies B Company also with an anti-tank gun and machine gun. Around Red Farm on the extreme left can be seen A Company and, although only one Sherman tank can actually be seen, there is another one in the· shelter of the Farmhouse. Also at the Farm is a mortar team with an observer; there is an artillery observer for off-the-table artillery situated behind B Company. Forward on Copse Hill are C Company with an anti-tank gun and a machine gun amid the trees. Immediately behind Copse Hill is a mortar team dug in, with their observer in the trees forward with the infantry. Behind the western end of Copse Hill the third tank of A Squadron 3rd R.T.R. is positioned.

The Germans have split their force—on their left flank (on the immediate far right of the plate), they have three tanks and three half-tracked personnel carriers with one complete infantry regiment (30 men). Covering the right flank of this force is an anti-tank gun and two machine guns. On their right flank, the Germans have an equal-sized force hidden behind the Plantation, and west of the Embankment three tanks with a complete motorized-infantry regiment in trucks behind the Embankment. On the Embankment itself can be seen on the extreme left of the plate an anti-tank gun, further to the right is a machine-gun team and then two observers for the mortars in position behind the Embankment. In front of the Embankment is a scout car containing an off-the-table artillery observer. ·

The German intention is to advance their left flank first and outflank Copse Hill, getting round behind it. When this has been done and, it is hoped, some of the other British troops and reserves have been involved, the right-flank German force will go straight for the St James Road, past Red Farm. (Note: Although it does not show up particularly well on the photograph, there is a very distinct slope rising up from the table in front of Copse Hill and in front of the barbed-wire apron between Red Farm and Copse Hill. This makes the British position difficult to attack and well chosen, which might not appear so in the photograph.)

Plate 12—The German left-flank attack makes headway
With their right-flank striking force holding fast until it could advance to best advantage, the German left-flank force achieved early success. Striking for the lightly protected British right flank, the three tanks leading, the force rapidly and smoothly carried out its allotted role. The first tank swung right to attack C Company of the Guards on Copse Hill and a half-track debussed its infantry to attack the eastern edge of the Hill. The second and third tank moved forward, through the wire and then inwards behind Copse Hill; the second half-track disgorged its infantry, who attacked the flank of the Hill; whilst the third Company in their half-track moved through the gaps torn in the wire by the tanks, to debus well behind Copse Hill and in the face of HQ Company of the Guards (in reserve).

Owing to their position of facing directly forward, the majority of C Company in the wood on Copse Hill were unable to fire with much effect on the advancing German force, the British anti-tank gun in particular firing repeatedly to no avail. On the other hand, so well hidden were the British force in the trees that fire from the German tanks caused no early casualties whatsoever. The British mortar team behind Copse Hill did not succeed in scoring any hits on the German soft vehicles carrying infantry either.

The Sherman tank on the western end of Copse Hill swung round to cope with the sudden advance of armour in its rear but was immediately hit by the German anti-tank gun that had accompanied the armour, it brewed up at once and became a total loss before it had fired a shot. This was somewhat balanced by a good shot from the British anti-tank gun lying well dug in with the Guards HQ Company; this gun scored a hit on the right-hand Panther causing a penetration on the turret ring right of the gun: the tank immediately brewed up and became useless.

So far the German attack had succeeded in that it had out-flanked the British position, but although it had automatically involved the British reserve (HQ Company) the remainder of the British force had remained firm to counter an advance from the remaining German right-flank force. The British infantry on Copse Hill, although outnumbered and outgunned, were fighting back and causing casualties on the German infantry as they debussed.

Plate 13—The German right-flank force moves forward
It might be said that the German plan miscarried at this stage in that one of two things went wrong—either their left-wing outflanking force failed to move fast enough forward after their early successes or else the right-flank force began their advance before the time was ripe, in that the British left flank had not moved or lost anything in numbers or firepower.

With one tank out of action, another strangely hesitant in front of Copse Hill, the outflanking German force had only one tank behind Copse Hill and not many more infantry than had the British. In addition, there was a British anti-tank gun well dug in and flushed with its earlier success to be considered. The German infantry hung closely to the shadow of their armour and lost fairly heavily from the Guards HQ Company who retreated slowly back to form a fighting flank with survivors from Copse Hill which still had not been overrun by the far-from-dashing German infantry in their heavier numbers.

With no apparent attempt at co-ordination with their left flank, the German right-flank force moved from their start-line and roared across country towards Red Farm and the forward slopes. Immediately the British mortar had a partial success when it landed a bomb behind a personnel-carrying truck, killing some of its occupants. Some bombs from the German mortars landed harmlessly in the area of the British wire; these weapons had been sited too cautiously so that they had not got sufficient range to hit Red Farm or the Guards B Company, nor could they fire on the Copse Hill area for fear of hitting their own men.

One Sherman moved forward and received a glancing hit

from the right-hand Panther; this did no damage and the British tank, as though celebrating its let-off, scored a direct hit on the German tank, causing it to brew up at once. The other Sherman remaining under cover of Red Farm fired at the second Panther and missed, the Panther returned the fire and also missed. But the British anti-tank gun dug in between B Company and Red Farm did not miss—carefully waiting until the Panther exposed a portion of its belly as it climbed the last few yards of the slope, it scored a direct hit on this vulnerable area and a second German tank was out of action.

Evidently confused by the pall of smoke from the burning tanks, the German infantry in their left-hand personnel-carrying truck debussed too early so that they were on their own side of the British wire which had not been gapped at any place. Seeing them leave their vehicle, the infantry in the truck following the second knocked-out Panther also debussed, again on the wrong side of the wire, and began to move forward through the smoke.

Plate 14—The Guards strike back

The discomfiture of the German right-flank force continued, the Sherman positioned behind the Farm used its 75 mm gun to great effect when it scored a direct hit on the personnel-carrying truck on the German immediate right flank, completely destroying it with all its occupants. At almost the same moment the anti-tank gun again scored a hit when it repeated its earlier success by hitting the third Panther on its soft underbelly as it nosed over the crest of the forward slopes.

With all their armour gone, and two Shermans nosing forward threateningly, the German infantry on this flank felt their nakedness of armour very acutely and turned in retreat. A number of them boarded a personnel carrier and made off, whilst the remainder tried to get away on foot. The first Sherman, scenting victory, moved forward between the burning Panthers in pursuit of the truck, but unwittingly came into line of fire of the Panther that had been dithering around on the forward slope of Copse Hill and which had now turned towards the right flank, its gun traversed for action. Seeing the

Sherman sideways on to him, the German gunner let fly and scored a direct hit on the thinner armoured side of the Sherman, causing it to brew up very quickly. The second Sherman turned to its right and moved across the field towards the rear of Copse Hill, with the idea of countering the Panther that was threatening to completely outflank the Guards and, at the same time, be in a handy position to cope with the second remaining German tank on the other side of Copse Hill.

A firm British firing line had now been established facing almost directly south and, although taking losses, these men were causing considerable casualties to the German infantry as they advanced across the open ground and off Copse Hill. At the same time the Guards had gone on to the offensive and A Company had advanced down the forward slopes and were now crossing the open ground towards the Embankment.

Plate 15—The Germans pull out
It was now obvious that the German thrust towards the St James Road had no chance of succeeding, their armour was sadly depleted and they were too thin on the ground to be able to turn their left-flank feint into a telling attack. There was a sudden definite easing-off of the pressure on the hard-pressed British forces and they were heartened to see the Panther on the German far left flank back out, being missed twice by the anti-tank gun and completely missing with its own gun as it did so. At the same time the Panther that had done so little behind Copse Hill turned and began moving back towards the Embankment, unmolested because the anti-tank gun on Copse Hill had been destroyed and there were no further British heavy weapons far enough forward to be effective on the heavily armoured tank.

Leaving machine gunners and an anti-tank gun to cover them, the German infantry pulled out and moved back round the eastern end of Copse Hill, retreading their original path as they advanced earlier.

Both Panthers and a number of the German infantry got back to the safety of the Charlot Road Embankment, the pursuing Guards A Company coming under concentrated fire of the Germans' mortars behind the Embankment and being prevented from carrying on what would probably have been a disastrous pursuit anyway.

The position had been held and it was never again seriously threatened as the Guards were strongly reinforced that night by 2nd Battalion Coldstream Guards and the remaining three Squadrons of 3rd R.T.R., whilst the German forces withdrew some ten miles to conform to their general line on either flank.

Losses

British: 2 Sherman tanks, 1 anti-tank gun, 1 machine gun, 18 infantry (8 C Company, 4 HQ Company, 2 B Company and 4 A Company).

German: 4 Panther tanks, 1 truck destroyed, 2 half-tracks and 1 truck abandoned, 1 machine gun, 25 infantry.

9

Solo War Games

ALL war-games enthusiasts are not sufficiently fortunate to have opponents living conveniently within reach, so that they can fight and arrange mutually battles and campaigns. Many collectors live in areas in which they are the sole enthusiast, thus they either fight battles only when they go visiting other collectors or are themselves visited, or else they adapt themselves to fighting solo games.

The lucky player with his opponent residing within easy reach tends to patronizingly deride the solo game, to point out that it lacks any element of surprise and that a good game is impossible when one man knows both sides' tactics. Agreeing that there might be such a case put forward, nevertheless many war gamers thoroughly enjoy their solo games, and one very great enthusiast at least vastly prefers to play against himself—he says that there are no arguments.

It is possible to play ancient, horse-and-musket or the modern game solo—using the rules that have already been laid down in this volume—but, to ensure a good and interesting game, certain additions are required. By means of these items it is possible to re-create the element of surprise that the lack of an opponent causes; it is quite easy to find that the battle is slipping from the grasp of one side without any bias or favouritism being shown to either force.

Firstly, to get full enjoyment out of solo war games it would seem that it is vastly preferable to fight a campaign or series of battles, using maps and all the routines described in the chapter dealing with map campaigns. The player should obtain a master-map of the area or country over which he intends fighting (scale is not important and a touring map is often quite suitable). Next, tactical maps have to be made—these are larger in scale and consist of one very large map squared off into scaled-down 'tables'. Thus, the map might be of the area from Staunton to Winchester in the Blue Ridge Mountains of American Civil War memory. It will be divided into perhaps a dozen squares, each one being a war-games table; in other words a battle will take place on a terrain exactly as in one of these squares made up on the war-games table. The campaign will surge back and forth over this tactical map, with terrains being erected in accordance with the squares on the tactical map, the larger manœuvres being shown on the master-map.

Next, it is necessary to obtain a friendly correspondent who will dictate the tactics for your enemy—thus your war might be between Federals (your side) and the Confederates, who will be controlled by mail written by your opponent. He will be given both a master-map and a tactical map; you will both outline your general opening dispositions and your intentions; then the player will begin his map moves. When a contact is made, that terrain will be erected and a battle fought—the tactical instructions received by mail must, obviously, include both offensive and defensive instructions, in case the Confederates receive a reverse and have to withdraw to one other rear square on the tactical map. In this manner it is pleasantly possible to carry on a most interesting solo game, possessing many elements of surprise and frustration.

Should a live mail opponent not be available, then other steps must be taken. Carry on and plan the campaign as before then make out a whole series of Tactical Chance Cards, three sets: (a) Offensive, (b) Defensive, (c) Withdrawal. Each card bears general instructions for the army and its initial moves, decide which army is to draw an offensive card, and which one take defence—then draw the card for each force and carry out the instructions contained thereon for the first battle. It may well work out that the offensive side suffers defeat, and the next card it has to draw will be a defensive or withdrawal card, whilst the enemy originally on the defensive will now draw an offensive card. And so the game can proceed by each force carrying on its movements in accordance with the orders received from its high command on the Chance Card.

Another method, or an addition, is to also have a set of General Chance Cards, each one of which contains a situation which might well affect the course of the battle. For example, one card might say, 'Line of Communication cut by Partisans—no supplies for two moves during which time Army cannot move', or, 'Courier waylaid and killed, your right flank receives no orders and stays still for one move'. These cards to be taken whenever one certain thing occurs in a game; for instance if one general, when throwing his 'firing' dice for his riflemen, throws a *one*—for each *one* thrown he has to take a Chance Card.

A means of making life difficult during the actual battle lies in throwing a dice separately for each unit before it moves—if it throws a 1 or 2 it does not move that game move. A 3 or 4 means it moves normal distance that game move but a 5 or 6 means that it may move double distance that game move. An interesting means of starting a battle lies in declaring that 1 represents the right flank, 2 the right centre, 3 the centre, 4 the left centre, 5 the left flank and 6 the reserve. Before the battle begins, throw one dice for each unit—it may well work out that four units out of ten throw a 1, which means that the right flank is strong; two throw a 3, which gives two units in the centre; whilst two throw 6, which means they are in reserve; and two throw a 5, which puts them on the left flank. The enemy units work out that he has five in the centre, two on his left flank, one on his right centre and two in reserve. Thus, we have a line-up with uneven forces facing each other—immediately presenting a situation that calls for tactical thought. The reserve units must remain on the baseline until there is an actual contact made, either by fire or by hand-to-hand fighting, when they may move forward from the baseline in any desired direction.

One of the advantages of playing against oneself is that the battle can be started, left, taken up again and so on, provided the table can be left *in situ*, but even without this valuable

K

factor many original situations are open to the solo player. For example, he can begin a campaign realistically by having a small cavalry skirmish as the scouts of the two armies meet accidentally (as time is so valuable to war gamers who fight against each other one night per week, such a minor battle would never take place). Then it would develop into a larger affair as the advance guards of the two armies came up and take their place in the line; reinforcements would arrive, the conflict develop into a major affair, one side would begin to lose and then carry out a fighting retreat until its rearguard struggled to the end of the table bravely fighting off the pursuing cavalry of the enemy. All this might take many weeks, fitted in with odd evenings, an occasional Saturday afternoon when the local football team are playing away, one or two odd half-hours during lunchtime, etc., etc.

There are so many original ideas possible to the solo player that it need never be called dull or uninteresting. Tactical problems can be posed, left for cogitation, returned to, and generally browsed over in leisurely fashion. Solo war gaming is a most fascinating facet of the hobby and the collector who lacks an opponent need never be without his war gaming!

Appendix 1
Sources of Supply for Model Soldiers

IT SOMETIMES seems that the hardest part of war gaming is that concerned with the actual model soldiers and the artillery or vehicles, rather than the terrain over which they fight. Many would-be players are initially deterred by the difficulties they encounter in obtaining sufficient quantities of soldiers and accessories in a reasonable time and at an economic price. It is in an attempt to solve these problems that this section has been written. The world's principal suppliers of war-game, figures are as follows:

Great Britain

Airfix Products Ltd (toyshops, model and hobby shops Woolworths etc).

Douglas Miniatures, J. Johnston, 17 Jubilee Drive, Glenfield, Leicester, LE3 8LJ.

The Garrison, Castlegate, Knaresborough, Nr, Harrogate, Yorks.

Les Higgins, 52 High Street, Hardingstone, Northampton.

F. Hinchcliffe, 83 Wessendenhead Road, Meltham, Yorks. (Guns only).

Hinton Hunt Figures, Rowsley, River Road, Taplow, Bucks.

W. H. Lamming, 130 Wexford Avenue, Greatfield, Kingston-upon-Hull, Yorks.

Miniature Figurines, 5 Northam Road, Southampton, or 100a St. Mary's Street, Southampton.

Oscar Figures—Harry Norey, Longcroft, The Green, Little Horwood, Bletchley, Bucks.

Rose Miniatures, 45 Sundorne Road, Charlton, London S.E.7.

Tradition, 188 Piccadilly, London W.1.

Willie Figures, 60 Lower Sloane Street, London S.W.1.

U.S.A.

Command Post, 760 West Emerson, Upland, California 91786, U.S.A.

Hobby House, 9622 Ft. Meade Road, Laurel, Maryland 20810, U.S.A.

C. H. Johnson, P.O. Box 281, Asbury Park, New Jersey 07713, U.S.A.

Jack Scruby, Box 89, 2044 South Linwood Avenue, Visalia, Calif. 93277, U.S.A.

K. and L. Company (late Thomas Industries), 1929 North Beard, Shawnee, Okla. 74801, U.S.A.

Spain

Alymers Miniploms, Madestro Lope 7, Burjasot, Spain.

Sweden

Holgar Eriksson, Sommarrovagen 8, Karlstad, Sweden.

West Germany

Elastolin (O. and M. Hausser) Neustradt/Coburg, Jahreswende, West Germany.

Flat Figures

Aloys Ochel, Feldstrasse 24b, Kiel, West Germany.

Rudolf Donath, Schliessfath 18, Simbach/Inn OBB, West Germany.

F. Neckel, Goethestrasse 16, Wendlingen Am Neckar, West Germany.

Appendix 2

Rules for 'Close Wars'

IT IS difficult to reproduce in war games the type of fighting that takes place between small numbers of men in forests, such as in the French and Indian Wars of the late eighteenth century in America. Using about twenty-five or so troops on one side and about the same number of natives or Red Indians on the other, an exciting 'small' game can be played using the following rules:

The terrain must be crowded with material: strew large stones and pieces of rock round the table, make small hills, ridges and mounds, have meandering streams wind all over the table with plenty of bog and marshland. Have narrow paths through the wilderness, some of them ending in nowhere. Fill any bare spaces with pieces of twig to represent fallen logs and trees, have brush, bushes and trees dotted about in plenty, so that the entire table is a crowded maze.

Troops and natives both begin from their respective baselines, their objective being to seek out and destroy the enemy or to get at least 50 per cent of their force on to their enemy's baseline. They move at the following rates:

Natives, 9 inches.

Troops (in threes or less), 9 inches.

Troops (in greater numbers than threes), 6 inches.

Moves uphill are reduced by half.

Streams take 3 inches to cross.

Bogs and marshland can be deemed uncrossable or crossed at half-speed.

Moves on paths have 3 inches bonus.

Firing. Range is 12 inches *if* field of fire is clear. One dice is thrown for each man firing and a 6 scores a hit. If the firer is under cover whilst the target is in the open, then a 5 or 6 will secure a hit.

Each casualty has the chance of only being wounded and fighting on. Each man hit has a dice thrown for him, a 4, 5 or 6 means that he is only wounded and carries on. If the casualty is under cover then he is saved by 3, 4, 5 or 6.

Hand-to-hand fighting. Man versus man with each man having one dice throw, highest number wins. If numbers are uneven, then one man will fight two, three, or however many there may be with one dice being thrown per man, the single fighter kills all men who have dice throw lower than his own, whilst he is killed by higher dice throw than his own. Usual dice saving throws for mêlée casualties.

If opposing forces meet in a clear space, then a straight dice throw decides which force gains *impetus bonus*, which means that *one* is added to the dice score of *each* man on the attacking side. When a man or body of men emerge from cover to make an attack they are considered to have achieved an ambush and they automatically gain *impetus bonus*. On conclusion of mêlée, throw a dice for each side, multiply score by number of men remaining to give a morale figure, lowest score retreats *one* move directly backwards, dice being thrown to see if retreating force are routed (1, 2 or 3 denotes) or in good order (4, 5, 6).

Men attacked in flank or rear deduct *one* from their personal dice score whilst attacker automatically gets one added to his own score. Subsequent morale throw also deducts and adds *one* respectively for force being attacked and for attackers.

Appendix 3
Further Aids to War Gamers

MAN is a gregarious animal, learning from the advice and experience of others engaging in similar pursuits. War gamers are no different and the novice will find that his more experienced fellow-collectors are invariably quite ready to give him the benefit of their researches and experience. In order that the novice may know who these 'giants' are, and how he may contact them, it is suggested that he follows two courses of action.

Firstly, the majority of war-games players in both England and the United States of America subscribe to a monthly magazine *War-Gamer's Newsletter*, published by D. F. Featherstone, 69 Hill Lane, Southampton, SO1 5AD, England. In this magazine, the novice will find articles, hints, battle reports, new tactical ideas and the like, written by the subscribers themselves. He will also become familiar with the names of those most active in war gaming and will be able to contact them.

Secondly, he will benefit from the comradeship and activities of a war-games club. There are few people in Great Britain who live too far away from any of the established clubs listed below to be unable to attend their regular meetings. If you are one of these unfortunates, then why not start your own club? A notice in the local newspaper and in *War-Gamer's Newsletter* invariably attracts one or more people interested in the hobby. One bright lad began a very flourishing group by inserting slips of paper bearing his name and address inside copies of war-games books by Donald Featherstone in the local Public Library!

At the time of writing, the following list contained all the known war-games clubs and groups scattered throughout Great Britain. It is possible that others have formed since.

ABERDEEN WARGAME CLUB, David R. Allan, 58 Provost Fraser Drive, Northfield, Aberdeen, AB2 6LL.

BIRMINGHAM, SOCIETY OF WARGAMERS IN. Miss Vivienne Crabb, Mariemont, CBCE, Westbourne Road, Edgbaston, Birmingham 15.

BRISTOL WARGAME SOCIETY, M. Blake, 102 Cotham Brow, Redland, Bristol 6.

BRIGHTON WARGAMES CLUB, Tony Quatrine, 11 New Steine, Brighton.

CARDIFF WARGAME SOCIETY, Bill Cainan, 5 St. Mark's Avenue, Cardiff, CF4 3NW.

CHELTENHAM WARGAMES CLUB, Chris Beaumont, Hampton House, Shurdington Road, Cheltenham, Glos.

COLCHESTER WARGAMERS ASSOCIATION, R. G. Marshall, 1 Frensham Close, Stanway, Colchester, Essex.

DORKING KRIEGSPIEL SOCIETY, Stuart Etherington, 6 Dell Close, Mickleham, Nr. Dorking, Surrey.

DUNDEE WARGAMING CLUB, Sian Dunn, 1 Commercial Street, Dundee.

THE DURHAM WARGAMES GROUP, D. G. Sharman, Fawcett House, Broomside Lane, Belmont, Nr. Durham City.

EASTBOURNE WARGAMES SOCIETY, David Spencer, 70 Langney Rise, Eastbourne, Sussex.

ESSEX AND SUFFOLK WARGAMES CLUB, Geoffrey Kelker, Camelot, St. Jude Close, Parsons Heath, Colchester, Essex.

HARLOW WARGAME CLUB, D. O. Watson, 125 Hookfield, Harlow, Essex.

HORNCHURCH WARGAME CLUB, Henry Trevillyan, 96 North Street, Hornchurch, Essex.

IRISH MODEL SOLDIER GROUP, Ian Green, 14 Glenwood Avenue, Clonskeath, Dublin 14, Eire.

KNARESBOROUGH WARGAME CLUB, John Turnbull, 43 Woodpark Drive, Knaresborough, Yorks.

LEEDS WARGAME AND MILITARY HISTORY SOCIETY, C. A. Sapherson, 55 Wensley Drive, Leeds 7, Yorkshire.

LEICESTER WARGAME CLUB, T. J. Halsall, 8 Westleigh Road, Leicester.

LONDON WARGAME SECTION, The Secretary, 90 Burrage Road, Plumstead, London S.E.18.

MANCHESTER UNIVERSITY WARGAMES SOCIETY, Mr. Ley, c/o Moberly Tower Hall of Residence, Burlington Street, Manchester.

THE MEDWAY WARGAMES AND MODEL SOLDIER SOCIETY, Keith Ford, 374 Lordswood Lane, Chatham, Kent.

MERSEYSIDE WARGAMERS CLUB, N. J. Hunter, 8 Egremont Prom, Wallasey, Cheshire.

MID-HERTS WARGAMES GROUP, H. Gerry, 39a Sandpit Lane, St. Albans, Herts.

MIDHURST (SUSSEX) WARGAMES GROUP, Chris Speedy, 3 Elmleigh, Midhurst, Sussex.

NAVAL WARGAMES SOCIETY, The Secretary, 16 Hugo Road, London, N.19.

NORTH EASTERN WARGAMING CLUB, John G. Robertson, Upper Dunglass, Arbroath Road, West Ferry, Dundee.

NORTH LONDON WARGAMES GROUP, T. Fewster, 28 Huxley Place, Palmers Green, London, N.13.

OSWESTRY WARGAMES CLUB, P. Davis, Gable End, 1 Oakhurst Avenue, Oswestry, Salop.

OXFORDSHIRE PLASTIC MODELLERS GROUP, Oxford Model Centre, 94 St. Clements, Oxford.

PLYMOUTH SOUND NAVAL WARGAME ASSOCIETIA, B. J. Carter, Flat 14, Kirkby Fields College of Education, Kirkby, Liverpool.

RICHMOND WARGAME CLUB, Stewart Gordon-Douglass, 4 Enmore Court, East Sheen, London, S.W.14.

SEVERN VALLEY WARGAME SECTION, J. E. Hammond, 10 Richmond Road, Cardiff, South Wales.

SOCIETY OF ANCIENTS, P. Barker, 757 Pershore Road, Selly Park, Birmingham 29.

SOUTHEND-ON-SEA WARGAMERS, R. Cottee, 57 Moseley Street, Southend-on-Sea, Essex, SS2 4NL.

SOUTH SUSSEX WARGAMES CLUB, Malcolm Woolgar, 44 Shaftesbury Avenue, Worthing, Sussex.

SOUTH GLOUCESTERSHIRE WARGAMES SOCIETY, The Secretary, 24 Grange Park, Frenchay, Nr. Bristol.

THANET WARGAMES SOCIETY, The Secretary, 16 Princes Gardens, Cliftonville, Margate, Kent.

TUNBRIDGE WELLS WARGAME SOCIETY, George Gush, 154D Upper Grosvenor Road, Tunbridge Wells.

WALSALL WARGAMES CLUB, E. Stubbs, 22 Willow Road, Great Barr, Birmingham 22A.

WALTHAM FOREST WARGAME CLUB, The Secretary, 12 Warner Road, Walthamstow, London E.17.

WANDSWORTH AND WIMBLEDON WARGAMES CLUB, R. D. Stevenson, 4 Dyers Lane, Putney, London S.W.15.

WESSEX MILITARY SOCIETY, D. F. Featherstone, 69 Hill Lane, Southampton, SO1 5AD, Hants.

WORCESTERSHIRE WARRIORS ASSOCIATION, James Opie, Flat 2, Laurel Garth, 45 Graham Road, Malvern.

Appendix 4

Books and Literature Dealing with War Games

AT THE time of writing, the following magazines are published regularly and give a fairly complete and topical picture of the international war-games scene.

Airfix Magazine, Surridge Dawson and Company (Productions) Limited, 136/142 New Kent Road, London S.E.1.

The Bulletin of the the British Model Soldier Society, A. G. Clayton, 6 Hiliary Gardens, Stanmore, Middlesex.

The Courier, Bulletin of the New England Wargamers Association, R. Bryant, 45 Willow Street, Brockton, Mass. 02401, U.S.A.

Dispatch, Magazine of the Scottish Military Collectors Society, P. G. Pompa, 9 Viewforth, Edinburgh 10, Scotland.

Strategy and Tactics, Box 396, New York 10009, U.S.A.

The Vedette—The Journal of the National Capital Military Collectors, P.O. Box 30003, Bethesda, Maryland 20014, U.S.A.

The Wellsian Newsletter, Newell Chamberlin, 231 Westgate Avenue, St. Louis, Missouri 63130, U.S.A.

Slingshot—Official Journal of the Society of Ancients, P. Barker, 757 Pershore Rd., Selly Park, Birmingham 29.

Tankette—Miniature A.F.V. Association Magazine, M. Hundleby, 4 Lowcroft, Woodplumpton, Nr. Preston, Lancs. PR4 OAU.

The Armchair General, Post Office Box 274, Beltsville, Maryland 20705, U.S.A.

Tradition—The Journal of the International Society of Military Collectors, 188 Piccadilly, London W.1.

Battlefleet—Journal of the Naval Wargames Society, W. E. McKenzie, 16 Hugo Road, Tufnell Park, London N.19.

Bayonet—Journal of the Horse and Musket Society, Hamish Fraser, 27 Ramsgate Road, Margate, Kent.

The Canadian Wargamer, J. Hutchings, 4578 Brentlawn, Burnaby, B.C., Canada.

Guidon, Blair C. Stonier, 2555 Haverford Road, Ardmore, Pa. 19003, U.S.A.

Soldier Magazine, 433 Holloway Road, London N.7.

Milihistriot, Bob Bard, Box 1463, Baltimore, Maryland 21203, U.S.A.

Miniature Warfare, 61 Benares Road, Plumstead, London, S.E.18.

The best-known books on war gaming are:

Little Wars, H. G. Wells (1913) (Re-published 1970).

Wargames, Donald Featherstone. (1962).

Wargames in Miniature, J. Morschauser. (1963).

Naval Wargames, Donald Featherstone. (1966).

Air Wargames, Donald Featherstone. (1967).

Charge, Brigadier P. Young and Lt-Col. J. P. Lawford. (1967).

Advanced Wargames, Donald Featherstone. (1969).

Discovering Wargaming, John Tunstill. (1969).

Introduction to Battle Gaming, Terence Wise. (1969).

Wargames Campaigns, Donald Featherstone. (1970).

Battles With Model Soldiers, Donald Featherstone. (1970).

The following publications will aid the war gamer to assemble his table-top armies.:

Making and Collecting Military Miniatures, Bob Bard. (1959).

Model Soldiers: A Collector's Guide, John Garrett. (1960).

Lead Soldiers and Figurines, M. Baldet. (1961).

Model Soldiers, H. Harris, (1962).

Model Soldier's Guide, C. Risley and W. Imrie. (1964).

Tackle Model Soldiers This Way, D. F. Featherstone. (1965).

Collecting Toy Soldiers, Jean Nicollier. (1967).

Model Soldiers, R. B. R. Nicholson. (1967).

How to go Model Soldier Collecting, H. Harris. (1969).

Handbook for Model Soldier Collectors, D. F. Featherstone. (1969).

Military Modelling, D. F. Featherstone. (1970).

A History of the Regiments and Uniforms of the British Army, R. M. Barnes. (1950).

British Military Uniforms, W. Y. Carman. (1957).

European Military Uniforms, Paul Martin. (1963).

Military Uniforms of the World, P. Kannick. (1968).

Le Costume et les Armes des Soldats de tous les temps (Vols. I and II), Fred and Liliane Funcken. (1968).

L'Uniforme et les Armes des Soldats du Premier Empire (Vols. I and II), Fred and Liliane Funcken. (1968).

Cavalry Uniforms of Britain and the Commonwealth, Robert and Christopher Wilkinson-Latham. (1969).

French Army Regiments and Uniforms, W. A. Thorburn, (1969).

Appendix 5

The Lionel Tarr Periscope

How many arguments occurring during war games would be solved or even avoided if it were possible to take the place of the gunner behind his 30-mm-scale cannon, or get into the turret of the OO-gauge-scale tank and ensure that the claimed target is actually in sight? How many times have we felt that it would be possible to fire upon that body of infantry by the side of the old church but our opponent, with an indignant snort, denies that we can see them?

Bristol war gamer Lionel Tarr, who specializes in modern warfare, has discovered a method of getting the same view of a target as the gunner behind the gun or in the tank turret and, by means of his ingenious innovation, he has brought a note of realism to his game that is of a very high order. In Lionel's own words: '. . . I use a periscope—in reverse—to view everything from eye level so that my vision is exactly the same as that of the model; in this way I can stalk a tank with a bazooka, for example.'

The normal principle of a periscope is that, by its use, the holder can look into an aperture at his own eye level and obtain a view some feet higher or, in fact, as high as the height of the actual periscope—he could stand on one side of a seven-foot brick wall and look through his periscope to see a clear view of the other side of that wall. Tarr reasoned that if the mirrors in the periscope were reversed one could look through the top aperture and, by means of the bottom mirror, have a view at ground level from the point at which the lower aperture stood.

This apparatus is not difficult to make—a wooden or cardboard tube about 9 inches to 12 inches in length, at each end of which is cut an aperture about 1 inch wide and running the whole width of the tube (one aperture facing forward and one back). Inside the tube two strips of mirror glass are fixed, the top piece facing downwards and backwards, the lower piece facing forwards and upwards. Thus the view is obtained through the lower aperture and reflected in the lower mirror upwards so that it is caught by the upper mirror and can be seen by the viewer looking through the upper aperture.

To use the periscope, the viewer places the bottom of the tube lightly on the top of the tank turret, gun or even a man's head, and pointing in the direction in which it is desired to view. By looking through the top slit it is possible to obtain the same view that would normally be obtainable from ground level, as if the viewer were himself only 30 mm or so in height.